How to Choose THE ONE

By
Ardyce Rooney Grant, Ph.D

Para mi amiga carmen! con cariño Nelly 6/26/02

For Nelly Ardyce Grant

Llumina Press

ISBN: 0-9718509-3-3

Printed in the United States of America

This book is dedicated to the optimistic singles who believe anything is possible, to people who are now married and have questions about themselves and their existing mates, and to all those who have been previously married and are thinking about taking a chance again.

ACKNOWLEDGMENTS

Many people have helped to inspire this book: each and every single married and divorced client who was interviewed. Each has his/her own story. In sharing their experiences with me, they gave me a unique prospective on a complex issue and the knowledge to better help others.

I would like to thank Rose Ann Leonard, my sister Pat Dalla Rosa and Suzanne Coleman for their skillful editing work.

My thanks to the following people who made suggestions regarding some of the ideas in the book: Betty Weichert, Jim Morris and Fred Anglim.

Lastly, I owe a special debt to my daughter, Elisa, who was there from the beginning. Her youthful perspective was clear and her observations on target.

CONTENTS

INTRODUCTION

If you were told you only had a 50% chance of being successful at a lifetime career, you probably would not take the job. The truth is that couples marry 365 days a year with those same odds against them. To embark on a lifetime relationship with only a 50% chance of success is daunting indeed, and yet of the many couples who marry every day, half of them will face divorce within nine years.

In over twenty years of marriage counseling I have interviewed hundreds of couples suffering from various stages of anger, frustration, pain and loneliness. Despite professional help , many of these marriages failed.

What is the answer? Can a couple fight these odds? Is there a way to avoid a marriage doomed to end in divorce and the terrible sense of failure that accompanies it? I think so.

I never "saved a marriage" or advised anyone whether or not to marry the partner of his choice or to divorce a seemingly incompatible one. For the most part advice falls on deaf ears, especially when it comes to love and marriage. It is just easier to help people help themselves.

Over and over in my practice I listened to many unhappy couples echo the same message: "He changed so much after we married," or "She's not the same person I enjoyed dating."

In seeking a common thread to explain why these apparently dramatic personality changes occurred after marriage, I noticed that the greater the difference in a couple's personalities before marriage, the stronger the likelihood that the marriage would end in divorce.

Personalities are not drastically altered by marriage. Daily married life simply brings out personality traits in a manner not revealed in the unreal world of dating and courtship.

The old saying that opposites attract is true. But it is equally and unfortunately true that opposites do not make compatible marriage partners. In fact, the more two people differ in certain areas, the greater their chance of failure in marriage. Despite a strong initial attraction to an opposite personality, as the months and years pass, the initial loving relationship turns into a daily struggle to meet separate needs and maintain individuality.

These pages concern six practical steps of a self-help approach to make complex decisions about how to choose ***THE ONE***.

There are down-to-earth examples about individuals who briefly met, stayed awhile or became a permanent part of my clients' lives. This book explores compatibility, not merely through the infatuation of a chance meeting or a brief encounter, but from the experiences of those who have felt the pain of fighting the odds with a near-match or mismatch to his own personality.

Six compatibility factors are put forth for the single, married or divorced. Each and every part of a MATCH process is systematically explored. If an individual wants to avoid being doomed to years of unhappiness with his psychological opposite this book offers a workable compatibility model.

These pages contain stories of friends, lovers and spouses who were shocked to see their relationships failing, who could not believe that the love, contentment, comfort and happiness they had anticipated were steadily disintegrating. Moreover, these individuals had nothing to prepare them for the ultimate shock of the so-called change in their partner. With little to fall back on, they remained puzzled over the seeming lack of a reason for the "failure." Once they discovered the basis for their mutual incompatibility, the guilt began to lift, the anger subsided and the frustration gradually disappeared. They more rapidly came to terms with the beginning of the end. They were able to distinguish between their actual needs and those of their partner, grasp the true impact of critical areas of incompatibility and cope with an uncertain future.

For the single couple seeking premarital counseling the same six evaluators served as a yardstick to compare their personalities and needs to the MATCH formula. Hopefully, this would help them to ward off the mistakes of those married couples who were divorce bound.

For the individual in divorce counseling the six criteria were used to explain probable causes for the demise of his marriage. Finally, and by no means the least important, it would, hopefully, allay their fears about future relationships.

How do so many people who sincerely desire successful relationships nevertheless find themselves with incompatible mates? The simple fact is that the individuals were never really compatible in the first place, especially in the crucial areas I will discuss in succeeding chapters.

Many reasons are put forth in theorizing why a relationship fails, but separation is rare for two people who are genuinely compatible in certain critical areas. I do not mean to imply that compatibility, as I will define it, will prevent difficulties from arising, but it will provide a formula for choosing a lifetime partner.

Admittedly, men and women have different social influences. However, I found that for both groups that their scores fell along a continuum for sociability and communication. Moreover, equal numbers of men and women scored both high and low on each factor.

All of the names and pertinent details of the individual case studies included herein have been changed.

To minimize confusion, "his" is used throughout this book in the generic sense to include both men and women. (Language takes precedence over feminism!)

Chapter 1

There's No Such Thing As a Loser

"Don't tell me people have to have similar personalities for a successful relationship!" The speaker was Alisha, a vivacious, self-assured young woman and she was responding to a speech I had just given in Reno, Nevada, appropriately famous as the divorce capital of the United States, In my talk, "MATCH Your Way To a Successful Relationship," I had explained that compatibility and psychological similarity go hand in hand. While opposite personalities are attractive because they seem to embody all that we lack, to complement, fascinate and excite us at the outset of a new relationship, as marriage partners, it could prove disastrous.

"You mean to say that for people to be happily married they must have only *two things* in common, sociability and communication?" Alisha argued. "Isn't that putting it too simply, Dr. Grant? I don't agree with you at all! I just met a wonderful, charming man eight months ago . . . Jon and I are as different as night and day. He's the strong silent type, a private person who likes a lot of space. But I don't mind, it gives me time to do my own thing. I'm on a bowling team, president of my alumnae association and work out in a gym once a week. We're getting married May 1st!" Alisha smiled broadly and walked away, chatting to a group of friends.

Six months later Alisha left Jon, telling her friends she was filing for divorce. What happened to the perfect marriage? In a short time, "wonderful, charming Jon had turned into a "boring person" who was satisfied to sit home in silence with books and television. But Jon had not changed at all. His quiet, reserved personality was simply not compatible with the energetic, outgoing personality of Alisha. Because they did not *match* in sociability and communication, their relationship failed. Unfortunately, Jon and Alisha may feel that they themselves failed, that they are "losers", as our cruel society glibly brands those who are unsuccessful. The truth is, there are no "losers" in marriage, just those who have personality traits which match and those who do not.

For a long time I have thought about Alisha and all the Alishas who ever married who believed at first that differences don't create problems. Certainly most couples who marry are sure their union will last forever. Then why doesn't it? Everyone wants a successful relationship, whether dating, going steady, engaged or married; but what happens between dating and the exchange of marriage vows? As people who come to me for marriage counseling have echoed many times, it seems as though a person somehow changes and is different after marriage. Does one partner change, or does the other partner miss or overlook certain personality cues? Can people such as Alisha and Jon come to understand themselves well enough to accurately appraise their personality types before embarking on a foredoomed marriage? Certainly! This appraisal is twofold. Each partner must first know himself and his own needs, particularly in the critical areas of sociability and communication. Secondly he must come to understand his partner and his needs. Alisha and Jon had opposing needs. One wanted to be on the go, actively engaged in social events; the other wanted to be at home watching TV. One wanted to talk, and the other to read. The dissimilarity in their personalities and needs soon drove them apart.

There is no such thing as total similarity. Later we will discuss ways in which couples who differ in personal habits and interests can preserve their relationship. But the basis of every successful marriage is a blending of physical attraction, psychological similarity and love.

Since marriage is the commingling of two personalities, how do the differences in personality affect the relationship? If it is true that opposites attract, can they survive together? Let's take a look at this scenario.

Kira: "Don't forget Jim and Carol's anniversary party is Friday night."

Scott: "Another party. You know I don't like to go out on weekends. I wanted to rent a movie."

Kira: "We have to go. We missed their last two parties. You've changed since we began dating last year. You used to want to go out more. We never missed a party on a Friday, Saturday or Sunday. What's wrong with you lately?"

Scott: "You've changed too. Before, you couldn't wait to be alone with me and hugging and kissing went on for hours. Now you don't . . . Oh well, what's the use."

Kira: "Do whatever you want, Scott, but I'm going to that party Friday night with or without you."

What are Scott and Kira telling us about themselves? What are they really telling each other? To an untrained observer, Kira and Scott are just another couple spatting or having a lover's quarrel. To a professional, they are a classic example of clashing personalities. The message is clear: Kira enjoys socializing more than communication; Scott enjoys communication more than socializing.

Kira and Scott are opposites in two critical areas which form the foundation for lasting marriage: socialization and communication. But it is precisely in these two areas--socializing with others and communication between partners, both verbal and physical--that the deadly hazards to marriage most commonly occur. The major complaints are pathetic clichés:

> "You never take me dancing anymore."
>
> "We haven't been out together in six months."
>
> "We only talk during TV commercials."
>
> "Between football, baseball, hunting and fishing season I might as well be a widow."
>
> "After working, eating, sleeping, watching TV and playing with the kids, he has no attention left over for me."
>
> "She spends all her time at the mall instead of at home."

How much time do we spend weighing the superficial characteristics of a potential mate--the blue eyes, the red Corvette, the smooth line of patter, the fashionable clothes--only to overlook, as Alisha and Jon or Kira and Scott did, his partner's capacity for socialization and communication.

People at opposite poles of the sociability spectrum are all around us. Where do we find the high energizers? They are on bowling teams, leading club meetings, at every party, wedding and family gathering. They do not make excuses or turn down a social invitation unless they are running a 103°

degree temperature. If they accidentally find themselves at home, they are on the phone visiting their friends. The low social energizers are home quietly tending their gardens, repairing cars, knitting baby booties and blankets, working on creative hobbies, cooking all the latest bake-off recipes and reading. If you need to reach them on the phone or want to visit, they are readily at hand.

Those who were raised in an environment where the social milieu centered primarily around home and family activities anticipate that their adult lives will be a continuation of the same life style. Why not? Others who grew up with constant activity outside their homes unconsciously look forward to spending a large portion of their social energy away from their homes. Is it any wonder that where two people have different social expectations, a tug-of-war ensues? The high energizer favors activities away from home. The low energizer is an advocate of homebound activities. The high communicators are sharers. The low communicators keep their thoughts and feelings to themselves.

Differences in the areas of socialization and communication stem from parental personality patterns and:

- Cause daily conflicts in relationships
- Lead to the breakdown of close relationships
- Are reported by individuals as the major contributing factor in separation and divorce

Two people fall in love, are swept along by their romantic feelings, and pledge each other a lifetime of devotion in marriage. Only after the honeymoon does the cold light of reality dawn. When the courtship personalities are traded for the everyday personalities, incompatibility begins to undermine domestic bliss.

Would a systematic and realistic evaluation of a potential partner (and of oneself, or course) increase the possibility of choosing a compatible lifetime mate? Yes, it would! True friends are those who accept you as you are without trying to remodel your personality to suit their needs. The sweet devotion that accompanies most couples into marriage will slowly sour in the face of weeks, months and years of clashing personalities. Think of any two people of your acquaintance who recently divorced. Were their personalities in accord? Was one more outgoing and sociable, while the other preferred privacy? Was one more talkative, while the other enjoyed meaningful silence?

Dating *can* become the time to assess a partner's personality rather than reserving this crucial exercise until after marriage, when it may be too late.

Couples do not marry with the intention of divorcing or leave at the first sign of dissension. Admittedly, some do marry with either the intention of changing the other person or with an inkling that this relationship may not meet his needs. Some merely give into the pressure of outside forces such as family influences, pregnancy or financial security. Others may marry because they feel time is running out and this particular partner may be the last available choice. Mate selection is often based on either physical attraction or superficial qualities rather than on those factors that will insure one's chances for success and happiness. How many men and women choose a partner because he/she:

- Is good-looking?

- Is a nice person?

- Comes from a good family?

- Has sex appeal?

- Is a lot of fun?
- Has a promising future?
- Is someone who will take care of me?

Is it any wonder that half of modern marriages end in divorce? But then, who has time to ask the important questions when she is looking into big, blue eyes and a Brad Pitt smile, or he is embracing a curvaceous Cindy Crawford? Unfortunately, the turn-off usually does not come until after the wedding announcements are out and the down payment on the reception is made. Who can evaluate the more permanent qualities for compatibility when a marriage is a ceremony and a social event rather that the process of choosing a compatible mate for a lifetime? Over many years in innumerable sessions of marriage counseling, I have heard the same chorus of complaints:

- "If I knew then what I know now, I never would have married in the first place."
- "Why didn't I think of that before I married?"
- "By the time I realized she wasn't going to change, it was too late."
- "I know we were different, but I didn't think it would make any difference."
- "I saw him in one way--my mother, my father, my friends in another way, but I was totally blind to everything they were telling me. I guess I didn't think."

Few people would deny the importance of the need for a selection process based on reality rather than pure emotion; however, most people are not comfortable with premarital evaluations. Some of the discomfort arises from a general resistance to the ancient custom of match-making. In a democracy, freedom of choice is deeply cherished, and anything that takes away from one's basic freedom is met with opposition.

The public is bombarded yearly with books on instant analysis of your personality, dreams , fears, and how to improve your appearance, sex life or your marriage. While we try to climb to new heights with these hypnotic volumes covering all aspects of our personal lives, here is a "how-to" book for singles who have not yet made their final choice of partners, for divorcees who fear their next partner may become another disappointment, or for those who are already married but are curious to learn whether they were fortunate enough to have chosen a compatible partner.

It does not matter what you do for a living, how much education you have had, how many times you have been married or divorced--there seems to be universal interest in the topic of selecting partners. We all want to learn more about making this decision that extends until "death do us part".

In this book I hope to demonstrate that personality differences are a major factor in divorces. If you have ever experienced the frustration of being trapped in a relationship where both partners were emotionally engaged in a futile personality struggle, the subsequent chapters would provide straightforward information which will enable you to better evaluate future partners. If you have ever had a boss, mother-in-law or next-door neighbor who constantly rubbed you the wrong way, then you already know how it feels to have a partner who does not match you! It is not so difficult to accurately assess another person's actual needs and personality, but the process does require an honest, objective judgment. The factors I recommend as the basis for this appraisal comprise my match system:

M: Mirror image: a similar personality type.

A: Activity level: an equal interest in socialization.

T: Talking and touching: a corresponding need for verbal and non-verbal communication.

C: Compromise: cooperative decision- making.

H: Harmony: mutual acceptance.

We will look at each of these MATCH factors in our effort to make the selection of a marriage partner an honest and reasonable process. If we can take the time to consult *Consumer Reports* on the comparative merits of a contemplated refrigerator or a VCR purchase, then why not expend as much effort in selecting a lifetime mate?

Chapter II

<u>MATCH</u> Your Way to a Successful Relationship

Some years ago a song writer coupled "love and marriage" and even went so far as to state that they "go together like a horse and carriage". But what the writer failed to say was that physical attraction, which draws two people together like magnets, is a fundamental ingredient of both love and marriage. This chemistry test by which potential partners communicate through body language alone should be passed with high marks because it cannot be studied or taught after marriage.

You can change your hair color or make-up, get contact lenses or a face lift, and yet it is still possible to discover that your partner does not find you physically desirable. This is the crux of many more conflicts than we care to acknowledge. To desire and not be desired leaves a partner with the feeling of being a roommate or a boarder or, even worse, with a feeling of being shut out as the door closes. The emptiness of unrequited love leads many a partner into extramarital affairs, chronic depression and stress reactions. As one young client, Ryan, told me: "Heather is like a sister to me. I tell her everything and she tells me everything. I like her as a person, but our love life is worse than a second-rate movie! I keep hoping it will get better."

Neither love without physical attraction or physical attraction without love is a workable arrangement. One of the best ways to discover whether you find your partner desirable is to read this check list.

1. Do you feel a fascination for your partner which includes a desire to talk to him and be in his company?

2. Does your partner "turn you on" physically?

3. Do you find yourself wanting to reach out and touch your partner when you are in his company?

4. Do you have a tendency to think frequently about your partner?

5. Do you want to see your partner often?

If you are expecting to progress from meeting Mr. Wonderful (even if he does pass your chemistry test with high marks) to living happily ever after with no stops along the way, you are already in difficulty. While he is sweeping you off your feet and you are telling yourself there <u>is</u> such a thing as "love at first sight", you are failing to take into consideration whether as a couple you have those mutual personality traits which will help both of you to actually live happily ever after.

Dating is a period when each partner is customarily on his best behavior. As intimacy grows during this time, so does the sense that each partner is getting to know the other better and better. But dating or courtship is a fantasy land in which only the tip to the personality iceberg is visible, and the attractive tip at that; still submerged is the vast and substantial area of personality which will reveal itself after marriage. Thus so many people find out too late that they never really got to know their partners before marriage. Mitchell, a recent divorcee, told me: "I sensed that Tina wasn't my type, but I didn't know that could make or break a relationship."

My clients Alex and Andrea met at their local laundromat. She had been divorced one year; he for two years. The chemistry was there as they exchanged smiles and pleasantries. In between the wash and dry cycles they engaged in small talk. After all the clothes were neatly folded and tucked away in the cars, they continued their talk over coffee. They found that he golfed; she liked golf. He played in a band; she liked to listen to music. He said his marriage broke up because his wife did not like him away from home at night; she said her marriage broke up because her husband was a "workaholic" and was gone twelve hours a day. Over the next ten months Andrea and Alex golfed during the day, and three evenings a week she went to the club to listen to his band.

They married in June and came to talk to me the next June, two days after their first anniversary. Alex told me: "Our problems began when Andrea started working. We seemed to have a lot in common. When we dated Andrea was in my club three nights a week; after four months of marriage it dropped to once a week, and now she never comes near the place. I seem to be back where I started." Andrea told me: "Being married to Alex is worse than being married to a workaholic. At least the workaholic comes home at the end of his day!"

There are no shortcuts in selecting mates! If you stop after the chemistry test, as many often do, you will more than likely end up as a statistic in your local newspaper with Mitchell and Tina and Andrea and Alex under Dissolutions (another marriage nobody wants).

How do you get what you want in a mate? To be sure, being in love is an ecstatic state; however, there are avenues for separating the emotions and physical attraction from practical considerations without tampering with the fun of getting to know each other or the rapture of falling in love. Compatibility, reality and love can be blended in such a way as to assure a happy, comfortable, long-term bond if one goes into a relationship looking for common denominators. After the chemistry test, one first needs to be realistic about his own personality and then make a realistic personality appraisal of all potential partners. Do they or do they not match you? Without a formula, pairing is a haphazard process at best in which the odds are less than 50/50 for selecting your ideal mate.

Let us see how dating can be both entertaining and a time to search for answers about compatibility, matches and mismatches. To start your exploration, consider the following:

1. Do you feel that your personality is more similar than different from your partner's personality?

2. Do you have a corresponding need for socialization?

3. Do your needs to talk and touch approximate each other?

4. Do you have a tendency as a couple to meet halfway in making decisions together?

5. Do you feel harmony in the relationship?

If you answered "yes" to all five questions, chances are you have a match, if the chemistry is there. If you found yourself hesitating or saying "no" to any of the questions, chances are that you are in a relationship with a partner who could be what I call a "near-match". A majority of "no answers indicates you may be the type who is attracted to opposites, and the odds are you are mismatched. You may be drawn toward dissimilar personalities as a result of interaction with significant people from your past experiences.

Why are people attracted to a psychological opposite? First, to compensate for something he does not have. Some say, "I would be bored if we were too much alike." For them, somehow, more interest is generated with a dissimilar mate. Others may hold the belief that "variety is the spice of life". Others tell themselves they like the company of an opposite because there is never a dull moment. What they do not tell you about is the constant pressure of feeling as though they are walking on eggs. Each time he wants to be himself, his opposite exerts his personality too. "Didn't we already go out one time this week?", asks the homebody wife of the socially active husband. "We talked during dinner" (with the TV blaring in the background); "What more do you want?", says the reticent husband to the communicative wife. And so it goes, back and forth. Before you know it, first you are making an appointment with a marriage counselor and then with a lawyer.

My client, Kim, a pretty librarian, summed up her two year marriage with an opposite this way: "At first I liked socializing with Taylor. He sort of carried me along and tried to bring me out of my shell. I secretly hoped he would improve my social skills. Later I felt like I was in a race that I couldn't win. I got tired and felt I couldn't keep up with him. He was too popular and outgoing. I guess at first I wanted to be like that, but I don't think I would do it again!"

How one can hope to achieve compatibility by selecting a partner of opposite personality is a mystery. Then how does it occur so often? Every other marriage ends in divorce court. As long as individuals fall in love with their eyes closed to personality differences, the divorce rate will remain high. This is true even though young people are taking a longer time to select partners. The average age for young marriages is several years older than in the last decade. Admittedly, this may add to maturation, but maturation does not appear to be a reliable factor in choosing a mate. If it were, many older people would not marry and remarry as often as statistics show.

Those who are willing to risk a first marriage at a 50% chance of divorce need not accept these overwhelming odds. As you will see, you can become more successful in choosing your ideal partner.

If you think of the process of selecting a lifetime mate as so many steps in a ladder, desirability would be the first rung. After the chemistry test of physical attraction, these five evaluators are essential to assure that you have found a true match:

Mirror image: a similar personality type.

Activity level: an equal interest in socialization.

Talking and touching: a corresponding need for verbal and non-verbal communication.

Compromise: cooperative decision-making.

Harmony : mutual acceptance.

What is a mirror image? A mirror image is a person you understand especially well because his needs resemble yours in socialization and verbal and non-verbal communication. However, compatibility certainly does not require that two people are alike in all their interests.

The amount of social activity each partner enjoys is a critical evaluator in selecting a mate. It is of no importance if one partner is a highly social person or a private person--as long as both partners move at about the same social pace.

Since verbal and physical communication are of great importance in marriage, it is our third evaluator. It does not matter if both partners are talkative or quiet--as long as they are similar.

If compatibility exists in the first three areas, the couple who can also compromise and meet halfway in their decisions is more assured of a lifetime of give and take where needs are openly discussed and mutually satisfactory decisions are reached.

Lastly, a loving acceptance of the partner as he *is*, without alterations, is important. Mutual acceptance leads to a harmonious relationship in which two people who are physically attracted to each other can build a life together, socializing, communicating, compromising--*living* a successful marriage.

In the following chapters, we will look more closely at the ways in which these five evaluators of the MATCH System can contribute to a stable, permanent relationship.

Chapter III

Choosing a Mirror Image: Someone More like You

M:	**MIRROR IMAGE: A SIMILAR PERSONALITY TYPE.**

A: activity level: an equal interest in socialization.

T: talking and touching: a corresponding need for verbal and non-verbal communication.

C: compromise: cooperative decision- making.

H: harmony: mutual acceptance.

Choosing a Mirror Image: Someone More like You

Mirror, mirror, on the wall, who is the closest of them all? If choosing a partner can become a learning and loving process, then knowledge starts with examining what you find in your own psychological mirror, your road map to understanding compatibility. There is no question that psychological opposites are often attracted to each other. But these relationships become a matter of one mate attempting to pull the other in the direction of his own personality and needs. The more diverse the personalities, the deeper and stronger the conflicts and frustrations are for both. When the tug-of-war totally eclipses the relationship, divorce follows.

My client, Derek's story, an experience familiar to many, starts with the beginning of the end. He was 39 years old when his wife, Crystal, shocked him with her announcement at a family dinner that she was filing for divorce after 14 years of marriage. "How can you do this to me?" he thought. "I'm a good father." He had a close relationship with his two children, ten and seven years old. His first reaction was anger. After attempting to talk to Crystal, he found himself screaming threats to her. When Crystal called the police, Derek was asked to leave his home for a cooling-off period. That was the last time he lived in his home!

It took Derek three months of grieving--crying late into the night and drinking heavily to find some emotional relief. Going over in his mind every difficulty that he and Crystal had faced during the past year and reviewing every argument and every decision they had made, he felt there was no explanation for Crystal's insistence on a divorce. As his depression deepened, Derek's sleep fell to five hours a night, and his lack of appetite resulted in a ten pound weight loss. Finally, he arranged for his first visit in weeks with his children. When he arrived at the house, the children were with a babysitter who remarked that Crystal had gone out with her new friend. After a tearful visit and good-bye, Derek left.

Derek did not see his children for six more weeks. He was feeling angry at Crystal and angry at himself for not doing more to prevent the separation. As time passed, he was able to talk more freely and completely about the periods of discomfort he had experienced intermittently during his courtship and years of marriage. Crystal had always been a highly active person who was constantly criticizing Derek for his lack of interest in socializing with her. This had resulted in deep feelings of inadequacy and guilt on Derek's part over his inability to keep up with his wife. On the other hand, he had constantly felt frustrated with Crystal's lack of affection. He could recall many occasions when he would reach out to hold her hand or put his arms around her--only to feel her pull away, saying he was oversexed.

As Derek became more aware of how they had each struggled to obtain and maintain their separate needs, his feelings of frustration and anger lessened and his self-confidence increased. He began to accept the magnitude of the differences between their personalities which hampered each of them from being themselves. At the point when Derek realized he could never meet Crystal's needs or she his, he resumed a routine of seeing his children and attended a limited number of social events with close friends. Gradually his period of mourning and depression lifted, and he became reconciled to the reality that his marriage to Crystal was not feasible. As the months passed, he began to feel a sense of relief from the pressures of an incomplete marriage, and he settled into a more comfortable single life. At the time of our last talk, Derek stated that the self-understanding he had acquired would be helpful to choose someone more like himself.

In order to recognize your mirror image in another, you must, like Derek, come to know yourself and your built-in needs. The ideal time to do this is *before* becoming involved in a serious relationship--so that the sort of pain Derek suffered may be avoided. How much easier it is to take the time to evaluate your needs for socializing and for verbal and physical communication calmly and objectively before choosing a partner, thus sparing yourself the agony of years of daily wrestling with a partner who is least able to comprehend and appreciate you for what and who you are.

Childhood is an excellent starting point for self-evaluation. Each of us incorporates into his personality certain traits from one or both parents, however reluctant we may be to accept this idea. It is useful to determine which traits we may have acquired from which parent.

Of special significance would be a clear understanding of each parent's needs for socializing and communication. Was Mom reclusive and cool, while Dad was outgoing and warm, or vice versa?

Both men and women have said to me over the years, "Don't tell me I'm like my mother or my father." But we all have some of each of our parents traits within us. Sometimes the basis of an individual's depression in a marriage will be a feeling of discomfort and unhappiness when he finds himself reacting in a love relationship as one of his parents would have reacted. How often we catch ourselves mimicking a parent. We may order a spouse to "pick up your clothes." using the same expressions we heard as children. Marriage counseling so often reveals that a couple has inadvertently traveled back home, psychologically speaking, by re-experiencing the very same difficulties they recall from their parents' marriage. Why is this?

When you think about it, your parent's marriage was the first model that you had for marriage. For example: if your parent's marriage was the coupling of two psychological opposites in sociability and communication, you were taught to select opposite types.

We all need to understand our parents' choices more fully before making our own choice. For example, a sociable person with one reclusive parent may unknowingly choose an inactive partner only to re-experience the pain of his parents personality clashes. The more astute learn to avoid opposite types once they have observed personality clashes at home.

Since parental choices are a critical influence in choosing an ideal mate, the children of psychologically opposite parents may ironically be led away from compatible partners and toward an incompatible mate who cannot meet their expectations.

"My mother married four times," one perplexed 27-year-old woman in a third marriage said. "similar people bore me! I find people different from me more interesting and exciting since I never know what to expect from them." Can this cycle of choosing psychological opposites be transmitted from parent to child like a predisposition for diabetes or alcoholism? The answer, of course, is yes.

Those who are challenged by opposites face a profound revelation when they discover that they have not succeeded in changing their partners any more than their parents did. A man with unusual insight once told me what it is like to experience this phenomenon: "If I had ever realized my wife would end up acting like my mother, I would never have married her. It's scary. My mother and I were never close or friendly, and she always wanted more from me than I could give."

Those who grew up in a family where the parents were compatible and conflict was at a minimum would be wise to choose mates similar to their parents in sociability and communication. Those who marry opposites only to discover that their marriage parallels their parents'--that the personality conflicts and frustrations they were so keenly aware of as they grew up are now being recreated--describe the experience as a nightmare. A young woman told me, "I never thought my marriage would end up the same as my parents'. Now I understand why my mother and father argued day and night."

My client, Jessica ran out of patience with her mate, Larry, who only socialized after work while she was home trying to keep their evening meal warm and attractive. "I love him," she said, "but we never even eat a meal together. His companions are out there on the bar stools. I told him flat out it's over if he doesn't change his ways."

If your choice of an incompatible mate has not been predetermined by parental influences, the next most common way to mistakenly choose an opposite is to misread cues about your partner's dating personality. Dating is the time couples get to know each other. Even the most casual date leads to a greater knowledge of the other party, more facts about his background and interests, and a surer sense of his manners and temperament. Continuous dating of the same person--whether you label it "going steady" or the quaintly old-fashioned "courtship"--should be a period when a couple becomes thoroughly acquainted with one another, seriously evaluating each other as potential lifetime partners. We all know nothing could be farther from reality. As a new relationship blooms we are carried along on the tide of love, perceiving all that is positive and promising in the beloved and overlooking or rationalizing any flaws. Each partner strives to please the other, to be the person the other desires. In the warm glow of romantic love, the shy homebody attends weekend parties and the armchair sports fan becomes a touch-football player. The quiet man talks more and the energetic woman slows down to listen--all to please and accommodate the other person. No wonder most marry with the firm conviction that his partner has the same personality traits. But with marriage comes reality. Now the time has come to be yourself, to stay home or go out as it pleases <u>you</u> and not someone else. The rose-colored glasses hit the wastebasket and the new relationship is bathed in cold, harsh daylight. The real evaluation begins.

Endlessly over the years I have heard reiterated in dozens of ways this basic complaint: "As soon as we were married, my husband/wife changed." A dramatic example of this was Anthony, who told me: "When we were dating, Cheryl and I spent every moment on my sailboat, sailing and making love. After our honeymoon was over, she vowed she would never set foot on it again. I wonder what happened to that woman I used to know when we seemed to have so much in common? It's come to the point where we never see each other anymore."

Are you beginning to understand what I mean? In the basic boy-meets-girl date, it would appear that everyone happily shares interests and goes at about the same pace. After marriage, if one partner asks the other to participate in activities, the answer may be somewhat different: "We're married now. Do we have to be on the go all the time?" or "It's awfully late and every place will be crowded, or "I'm too tired. You go alone." At this point one of three things may happen. The sociable partner may gravitate toward his partners' need and stay home and thus put aside his true need for activity. Others alleviate their frustrations by starting to create excuses to go out alone: meetings after work; "getting together with the boys/girls"; working late at the office. Some unconsciously create conflicts on other levels, usually in the form of personal complaints such as "You didn't take out the garbage" or "You didn't iron my shirt" or "You didn't put the lid back on the toothpaste." This indirectly expresses anger toward a mate's inactivity which has stifled their social life or a mate's over-activity which leaves them home without a companion.

Husbands and wives who sense personality clashes early on in a marriage soon feel disillusioned. It is as if all the pleasure and companionship they found in months of dating have been snuffed out. Without companionship, intimacy and communication begin to deteriorate. Marriage entered into with such high hopes becomes a source of despair and failure. Anyone who has ever dealt with the frustration of living with a partner who is in discord with his needs will concur with my client Noelle, a realistic young woman who said, "I just want to be *me*! My husband and I were at odds in our social *and* sex life from the first day we married."

Why is it that a person accommodates himself to his date's personality, thereby creating an illusory compatibility? Perhaps it is done in the name of love, a willingness to make sacrifices early in a relationship, or a longing to have someone in your life. Love created the fantasy; marriage brings out the reality. Even in the most inspirational of love relationships, there ultimately begins the routine of a day-to-day married life. While waiting for the husband to take her dancing and whisper sweet nothings in her ear, the wife is mopping the floors, doing the dishes and sorting the laundry; and he is waxing the car, taking out the garbage and walking the dog. When reality sets in, you should not have any illusions about the type of person you married.

The need for a realistic evaluation of yourself and your potential partner *before* marriage is crucial. People do not change overnight from reclusive to sociable, from reticent to communicative, from frigid to affectionate. The romantic aura which surrounds dates leads us to behave differently than usual and to judge one another less objectively. The simple fact is that the more *similar* potential partners really are in the areas of *sociability* (mixing with others, participating in activities outside the home) and *communication* (talking, touching, expressing themselves), the more assured they can be of a lasting relationship.

There are many ways in which two people can differ that may cause minor disturbances but will not lead to divorce. Everyone has met an "odd couple"--the compulsively neat Felix who has the dirty ashtray or dinner plate in the dishwasher before you have finished using it, living with the Oscar, who can be found by following the trail of clothes and papers he has left behind. The patient man may marry the impatient woman. The eternal optimist who will always perceive the luscious doughnut may wed the pessimist who only sees the hole. These are problems which married people learn to live with, but they do not reflect incompatibility. God help us if all the neatnicks began to marry each other, leaving all the slobs to pair off! The planet would be doomed.

I do not mean to imply that total similarity is necessary for a successful marriage. There is always room for differences in interests, hobbies, personal habits and viewpoints; but in your search for compatibility, you should start with your *mirror image* in sociability and communication.

As you will see, you can discover ways to use all five evaluators in seeking out your ideal partner. If you like yourself, you will like the mirror image you are about to discover--someone like you!

Chapter IV

The "A" Factor: Your Secret Ingredient to a Long and Lasting Relationship

M: mirror image: a similar personality type.

A: ACTIVITY LEVEL: AN EQUAL INTEREST IN SOCIALIZATION.

T: talking and touching: a corresponding need for verbal and non-verbal communication.

C: compromise: cooperative decision- making.

H: harmony: mutual acceptance.

The "A" Factor: Your Secret Ingredient to a Long and Lasting Relationship

Sex sells, but is it the most important factor in mate selection? The answer is a resounding "NO"! The "A" Factor, which represents one's social energy, is your secret ingredient to assure a long and lasting relationship.

In this chapter we will discuss the second point in the MATCH System, which I call the Activity Level. Each of us has an Activity Level, or social energy which we channel in many different ways. Someone with a very low activity level is labeled as a homebody or a couch potato. On the other hand, a person with a high activity level would possess great social energy and would be termed outgoing or a real go-getter. Activity level does not mean a person's level of productivity, but of social involvement to the degree to which he enjoys being out of the home, engaged in independent social activity or in contact with others. For each of us our Activity Level (degree of sociability) is nurtured within the family in childhood, and these early patterns continue into adult life.

A marriage partner is first of all a companion, a built-in friend with whom to share activities. The more closely two partners match in Activity Level, the more compatible companions they will be over the years. They will share equal enthusiasm and interest in the many or few social activities and events which are part of their life. The greater the difference in partners' Activity Levels, the greater their incompatibility, usually manifested in misunderstandings and constant power struggles. Familiarity with your own and your potential partner's "A" Factor (Activity Level) is absolutely essential to choosing a compatible mate. To marry an opposite in this area is to stack the deck against yourself.

In the social realm there are homebodies and there are high energizers. Each can live happily and productively, if they MATCH. Marriage partners with widely differing Activity Levels invariably become locked in an endless power struggle. One wants to attend a gathering; the other wants to stay home and work or relax. While compromise is possible, neither partner would ever be true to his own personality needs. Whereas, partners with a similar Activity Level can handle their social life in a manner that is mutually comfortable and makes for an enduring union.

The homebody and the high energizer view the role of sociability in their lives in a completely different manner. While both can be very productive, the low socializer lives and works more quietly and has less need of a large number of people in his personal and social life. The higher socializer is more obviously outgoing (in both senses) and engages in a greater number of social activities. The world needs its extroverts and its introverts and all the 'verts in between to keep it balanced. The point is that we need to be aware of both viewpoints and to respect the preferences of each one. The private person who avoids many social commitments and the social butterfly whose engagement calendar is packed are equally normal. The problem arises when one type chooses to marry the other. Two opposing social viewpoints cannot live long in peace and contentment, let alone provide each other with any meaningful companionship.

Each couple's life consists of either two or three avenues for sociability. There are independent activities which one spouse participates in without the other. Then there are activities which husband and wife enjoy together as a couple. And finally, there are family activities which include parents and children. A well rounded social life should include portions of either two or, in the case of having children, all three of these social outlets.

In a troubled marriage, the manner in which the couple's social life is conducted is a major source of conflict. The independent activity of one spouse may lead to complaints by the other spouse because it detracts from family and couple time. Overemphasis on family activity may interfere with necessary time a couple spends together as adults. And the time two spouses spend together can only be enjoyable if they are in agreement about time spent either as a family or alone.

These complaints about the quality of companionship after marriage are typical:

> "All he does is go to work, sit in front of the TV and then go to bed."
>
> "All I hear is, "Let's go here', 'Let's go there."
>
> "Somewhere between dating and marriage I lost my social self."
>
> "I had the feeling that she was trying to draw me into a box and close the lid."
>
> "He stopped taking me out before we were married a year."
>
> "I was going to teach her to be social."
>
> "I didn't know he was *that* social."
>
> "When we met we seemed to have a lot in common; now something seems to be missing."

Unfortunately, most partners do not discover until after marriage that their varying Activity Levels have caused them to grow farther apart instead of closer together.

Rebecca and Aaron met in an Ivy League college where he lived in a highly social fraternity house and she was head cheerleader. After graduation they were married in an elaborate wedding. They honeymooned for two weeks in Europe; then returned to work, he as an executive in his father's accounting firm, she as a second grade teacher. Rebecca became my client after three years of marriage. She talked about a birthday dinner for Aaron for which she had invited five couples. Aaron arrived one hour late explaining he became absorbed in a computer program and "lost track of time". During the dinner Aaron's only words were a toast to Rebecca, "the perfect hostess".

Later at their townhouse, an argument followed. "Aaron, you didn't even make polite conversation with our dinner guests," Rebecca blurted out before bursting into tears. "I didn't feel like it," he replied.

She said that on each social occasion Aaron became "quiet and sulked" all evening. A few of their friends had begun to decline invitations from them of late. Rebecca found herself inventing excuses for his silence: "Aaron has a lot on his mind these days. He has a lot more responsibility at work since his father had his heart attack." Tearfully Rebecca talked about other social occasions and concluded, "If he doesn't want to go out with our friends, why doesn't he just say so?"

It became clearer to Rebecca that she was the initiator of all their social plans and that Aaron never suggested going anywhere. He seemed content to go to his office, work long hours, and then come home to a late dinner and TV. They talked it over and Aaron promised to curtail his work hours and actually began to be home earlier. And their social life? Aaron said, "I get all the socializing I need at work."

Rebecca tried a few changes in their social life. She planned dinners and card games in their home on the weekends. During the week she kept busy with school papers, household chores and reading. Aaron was doing exceptionally well and was promoted to Assistant Vice President. He loved his job and home. Aaron would like to buy a house, but Rebecca was afraid: "I already feel like I'm imprisoned, like a genie in a bottle! I don't see how having our own home would help that. If anything, it would keep Aaron home even more."

Rebecca remained in her dilemma for two more months, at which time Aaron's father died, leaving Aaron in charge of the business. At the time of our last meeting, Rebecca summarized her marriage situation by saying, "Aaron needs me more than ever now." But what about Rebecca's needs - for companionship, intimacy and social activity?

An equal interest in socializing is an important key not only to marital compatibility, but also to the mental health of each partner. An inestimable amount of marital conflict arises over the issue of sociability, from the simple decisions like joining a bowling team to weightier matters like attending the boss' formal dinner party. If one partner has a high Activity Level and really relishes a night out at every opportunity, and the other partner has a lower Activity Level and really cherishes an evening at home, one of the two partners is going to be short-changed in every social decision. No matter how much one partner wants to meet the needs of the other, in the long run the true social needs of each will prevail. Love cannot counteract this personality trait., The socially energetic partner will feel frustration, anger and guilt at his inability to engage his partner in what he perceives as pleasant social activity. These same feelings will burden the inactive partner because he does not share this enthusiasm for social activity and would actually prefer to be excluded. These disparities in socialization rarely become apparent before two people are married. During courtship, partners are more likely to mask their true personalities, and rarely show resistance until after the marriage bond is established.

Since social activity is basic to a happy and successful relationship, it is helpful to ask yourself certain questions about your social life.

1. Have changes occurred in our social life, especially changes which affect our "couple time"?

2. Are most of our activities family or independent activities rather than couple activities?

3. Do I allow myself time to maintain my own interests?

4. Do I maintain equal portions of couple, family and independent activities each week?

How does a couple's social life become unbalanced? In a childless marriage between partners with widely varying Activity Levels, such as Rebecca and Aaron's, the problem is clear. Regardless of the amount of sacrifice one or both partners make, the twain shall never meet. When a couple has children, still other complications arise. In some partners the duties of parenting become all-consuming, to the detriment of the marital companionship which is due the other partner. The Super Parent can never leave the children for a night out, lest some vague catastrophe should befall. We also have Super Spouse, who regards leisure time as couple time only, never considering that children need to be included in family activities now and then. This leads to children who feel neglected, if not rejected, and one partner who must compensate for the lack of attention from the other.

In all of these unbalanced social lives, couples spend long, bitter years waiting for a miracle that seldom occurs. A well balanced social life consists of time spent together as a couple, time spent together as a family and time spent on one's individual interests and hobbies.

Now let's see where you stand on this critical "A" factor. One of the best ways to become familiar with the "A" factor within yourself and others is to read over the following lists and develop a better understanding of those with high "A" and low "A" factors (social interests).

LIST "A"

1. Are you "always" on the go?

2. Is it easy for you to meet and make new friends?

3. Does free time without something to do make you feel anxious?

4. Do you feel enthusiastic about attending a new type of social gathering?

5. Do people say you seem to have a lot of energy?

6. Do you enjoy serving as an officer in your social organizations?

7. Are you considered outgoing by family and friends?

LIST "B"

1. Do you prefer to watch television rather than participate in a social events away from your home?

2. Do you look forward to coming home from work and to read a book or workout or engage in a creative hobby?

3. Do you enjoy your own company a great deal of the time?

4. Do your friends refer to you as a private person?

5. Do you find yourself making excuses to avoid social engagements?

6. Do you like quiet peaceful vacations?

If you responded more positively to List "A" then chances are you are average or above average in Activity Level. If you responded more positively to List "B", then you are most likely low average or low in Activity Level. The importance of your Activity Level is not whether you rate yourself high, medium or low, but the fact that you *use* your score as an evaluator to choose a similar mate. Two high Activity Levels can find marital bliss, and so can two low Activity Levels, but let a high and a low wed, and disaster is guaranteed.

Activity Level, then, is the measure of a person's sociability, the degree to which he enjoys after-work activities away from home, whether alone or with others, such as evening meetings, dinner out, a movie, a bowling team, or a private workout at a gym.

A wide difference in Activity Levels can doom a relationship from the outset, joining two incompatible people in a painful struggle to meet their divergent needs. Answer the questions below honestly, both for yourself and for your potential partner.

1. Do you and your partner prefer social involvement ?

2. Do you and your partner prefer seclusion?

3. Do you and your partner share an enthusiasm for socializing?

4. Did you or your partner leave a relationship in which there was serious conflict over a lack of socialization?

As pointed out earlier in this chapter, Activity Level is influenced by one's family background. Answers to the following questions by yourself and your potential partner will also help to determine your respective Activity Levels.

1. Did you and your partner participate in extracurricular activities in high school?

2. Did you and your partner attend school and then go directly home?

3. Are you and your partner from families that were always on the go?

4. Are you and your partner from families that preferred quiet evenings at home?

If you and your potential partner both answer "yes" to either numbers one or three or numbers two or four, the odds are good for permanence in your relationship. With this information you can now give a numerical rating to your own "A" Factor or Activity Level by asking yourself:

Out of the seven nights a week, how many activities outside the home would you willingly agree to attend on a regular basis? Bear in mind that the key phrase to weigh in this question is "outside the home". Simply put, you must ask yourself how many nights a week you are willing to go out, whether with your partner, a friend, a group or alone. Let us say you attend a meeting every Monday evening, work out every Wednesday evening, go out to dinner every Friday evening and bowl every Saturday evening. No matter whether you do these things alone or in the company of thousands, you are *outside the home* four nights a week on a regular basis. Thus your numerical Activity Level would be four.

Now consider your own social pattern and determine your Activity Level based on the number of nights per week you are willing to spend outside the home. Put an "X" in the box that best fits your social preference.

1	2	3	4	5	6	7

Since the "A" factor in your personality is determined in early childhood, neither you or your partner's rating will change after you exchange vows.

Once you have determined your own activity Level, you know the Activity Level that your ideal mate should have in order to match your personality. Do not choose a mate who scores more than one point above or below you. Remember your score and use it as a dating tool. At a chance meeting, or a brief encounter, you can always ask, using your own words, what another person's Activity Level is. The answer can be provocative and practical. It helps you to discover, up front, if a person who has passed your chemistry test has the secret ingredient to a long and lasting relationship.

The second major component of a compatible lifetime partnership is communication. In the next chapter we will learn more about communication and how to determine your own and your partner's needs in this area.

Chapter V

Talking and Touching

M: mirror image: a similar personality type.

A: activity level: an equal interest in socialization.

T: TALKING AND TOUCHING: A CORRESPONDING NEED FOR VERBAL AND NON-VERBAL COMMUNICATION.

C: compromise: cooperative decision- making.

H: harmony: mutual acceptance.

Talking and Touching

If you hope to be happily married, do not choose your psychological opposite as a lifetime partner. Happily married couples have physical desirability as well as a high level of compatibility in their needs for sociability and affection interwoven into the fabric of their relationship. Incompatibility in even one of these areas can trigger a chain reaction leading a couple through periods of emotional distance, frustration, separation and even divorce.

Helen,a sales clerk, was 24 when she married Peter. Around the time of their first anniversary Helen said to me: "Is there something wrong with me? I see other couples talking and touching in public. Peter says he doesn't like public affection, but he seemed to like it when we were dating. We were always intimate, if you know what I mean."

Dating can be an optical illusion. What you see isn't necessarily what you get. Just as it is possible while dating to become confused about your partner's Activity Level, it is equally possible to misconstrue his interest in affection (talking and touching).

To observe the intimacy between dating couples, the impression would be that most partners have a mutual and equal need for affection. Unfortunately, dating often just makes it seem so. In this area of talking and touching, as with social needs, it is essential to evaluate yourself and your partner carefully before marriage. Otherwise, like Helen, you may find yourself facing apparent personality changes in your partner before the wedding cake has grown stale and the thank you notes are mailed.

"The talking and touching stopped way before the wedding bills were even paid," declared one bewildered young client named Felice. "I read sex books, bought flimsy nightgowns, served candlelight dinners, but Gregory says after you've had someone around for awhile you don't need all that love stuff." Gregory means he doesn't need all that affection, but where does that leave Felice and others like her? Another client, Doug, stated, "I know she loves me, but she doesn't show it like I do".

Dating is a time for sharing interests together, and to enjoy the closeness of talking and touching. It's a make-believe world in which each person plays out his role. At times an individual's true needs for social activity and communication emerge, but all too often the very context of dating masks one's true needs and personalities. Dating naturally brings one's best foot forward, whereas marriage is a time for planting both feet firmly in the real world.

Thus, what is needed is a method to scrutinize the real personality rather than the dating personality. Each of us spends our childhood forming personality traits, thus we should first be thoroughly aware of our own personality, our own Activity Level and need for Talking and Touching. Only then can we possibly size up another person as a Matching (or mis-matching) personality.

A dismayed young man once talked about his painful post-marital experience with his wife: "I knew her when she was a loving and warm person. But I haven't felt cared about for a long time. She doesn't have a clue what I'm really like." Sad testimony to the personality changes that seem to occur between dating and marriage. It's the common chorus marriage counselors hear again and again: "We don't seem to have anything in common any more. I wonder if we ever did." But the fact is that personalities do not change, nor can they readily be changed. The reserved wife will not become demonstratively affectionate after pronouncing her vows, nor will the reticent husband be transformed into a conversational genius by the marriage contract. We are what we are. We just need to learn to recognize what the other personality really is rather than what he *appears* to be so that we can spare ourselves a lot of grief.

Communication in marriage, as in any partnership, is vital, and yet the manner in which each one of us communicates is different. To form a compatible union, two partners must share a similar interest in talking and touching. By similar interest, I mean that each person must enjoy verbal and physical communication to the same extent. That extent may be small or large as long as it is the same in both partners.

The mass media, through TV commercials, magazine articles, books and newspaper reports on the latest sex studies, bombard us with the message that everyone out there is living in a state of divine intimacy. Eventually we begin to believe that something is wrong with our lives if we are not involved in an ongoing, intensely intimate relationship, totally "open and honest," of course, and physically satisfying at all times. Life, however, is not a soap opera. There will always be those quite normal people who have less interest in physical and verbal communication. Many of them have come into my office to ask, "If I don't have a need to talk and touch all the time, is there something wrong with me?"

This soap opera approach in which the characters are constantly exchanging thoughts and feelings, projects a false image of personalities and disregards individual differences in the need for intimacy. In real life few men and women need an ongoing emotional exchange at the freeway pace of a TV show. Far too many people feel as though they are failures and a disappointment to their partners when they compare themselves to the stars of "Melrose Place" or the sexual giants of Harold Robbins novels. The disaster that occurs when one partner attempts to turn a relationship into a marathon talking session can be a detriment to any partnership. One insightful, reserved person related in counseling: "You don't know what it's like to live with someone who follows you from room to room chatting about everything they think and feel. At least with a TV or radio you can pull the plug."

A marriage counselor hears many negative messages from confused partners which indicate that two people with different communication interests are caught in an unhappy union:

> "He says I'm oversexed."
>
> "I don't have time to sit around and make small talk. I get enough talking at work."
>
> "He can't even keep his hands off me while I'm fixing dinner."
>
> "What does she expect me to do, just sit around and talk to her?"

A low communicator simply does not possess such an intense need for talking and touching as a high communicator. And a high communicator, due to his very nature, is unable to restrain his spontaneity, even though his great need to talk and touch overwhelms his partner.

How we handle intimacy stems from our childhood and the manner in which our parents interacted with us and between themselves. When I ask people to describe the communication between their parents, some say, "I never even saw my parents kiss." while others respond, "My parents were always warm an affectionate with one another."

Intimate verbal and physical responses transmitted from the first moment of life throughout one's childhood, form a fundamental part of emotional makeup. Thus it sets the stage for the ease or difficulty which one will experience with adult intimacy. The more intimate our parents were with us and with each other, the higher our need for warmth and affection. Conversely, with less parental intimacy comes a lesser need for adult intimacy.

Few people either need or desire constant verbal and physical attention. The point is that whatever the level of our need for talking and touching, it should be fulfilled in marriage.

Let two people who have the same need for intimacy marry, their needs will indeed be happily fulfilled. But let a high and low communicator marry and the tug-of-war begins. An individual who enjoys intimacy to a greater extent than his partner will quickly feel unloved, while the partner with the lower need for communication will feel catapulted from a quiet, comfortable world into apparent pandemonium of another's overwhelming needs.

Frequently it is not until some time after the honeymoon that problems with verbal and physical intimacy surface, since intimacy is a deceptive quality more freely indulged in by willing partners before and during the honeymoon than after.

Changes in her sex life after two and one-half years of marriage prompted Stephanie to make an appointment with me. "Jake is a good husband and provider. Our house is kept up beautifully and our lawns are manicured. But I feel alone in my own home. When I was growing up my parents always found time to talk and visit at the end of a day, usually over a cup of coffee at the kitchen table. Jake's parents worked different hours. By the time Jake finishes his household projects I'm too tired to stay up and by the time he comes to bed I'm asleep. Our friends say I should be happy with someone who is so good around the house, but I'm not!

What good is a perfect house if I can't share my life with my husband?" Stephanie continued tearfully. Eventually Stephanie came to understand that she expected the kind of intimacy from Jake that her parents always had, but that her husband was not as comfortable with or as eager for the same degree of intimacy.

As far as I know, Stephanie is still living in her house that doesn't feel like her home. And as far as I know, we are what we are because of the way we were reared, and marriage doesn't change that!

Once I observed a couple at a dinner during which no verbal exchange occurred for thirty-five minutes, and yet they later told me "We've been happily married for thirty-six years." Other couples described spontaneous gab fests in which they enjoy talking for hours: "Sometimes my wife and I stay up late at night to talk. I can't imagine living with someone I couldn't tell everything to," Joel said to me.

Successful communication between a couple is based on a mutual capacity for intimacy, regardless of the level of that capacity. The marriage of a high and a low communicator is foredoomed to disaster. The more the high communicator's need for talking and touching is frustrated, the greater his withdrawal from intimacy, which allows the low communicator to become even less responsive. The low communicator tries to ward off what seems like a steady stream of verbal and physical advances by his partner. And the pain this inflicts on that partner is epitomized by Melanie, a young divorcee, who remarked: "Not only did I resent always being the one to initiate intimacy, but to be turned down time after time greatly added to my frustration and resentment."

Dissimilar needs for affection can sabotage a relationship in the same manner as different needs for companionship. Both partners feel betrayed and deceived. The person with the high need views his mate as unresponsive, and those with lesser needs feel their mates should have more self-control. One perplexed young man told me: "It's like Dr. Jekyll and Mr. Hyde, the way Kelly was when I first dated her and after six months of marriage. I thought we had a lot in common, and now we don't seem to have much to say to each other."

The less intimate partner suffers equally in these mis-matches. He quickly feels overexposed to constant verbal and physical interchanges. Nicole put it this way: "I enjoy my quiet times, and I like my own company a lot. Jamie can't be left alone for a minute. I feel like I haven't had an hour to myself since we were married. It's like being closed in a room with no windows."

Most of us marry with the belief that love will last forever and that the passion in the relationship will continue over many years. However, if two people with differing needs for physical intimacy marry, ultimately the intensity of the physical excitement will decrease. The aloof and unattain-able person who is pursued as a challenge while dating often turns out to be an unresponsive mate after marriage.

"I knew who she was, but I didn't know who she was going to become," one astute young man, Denis, said about his ex-wife's rejection of his advances after six years of marriage. As his wife proclaimed that he was oversexed, he began to believe just that, even though it did not seem accurate. The husband's psychological reaction to this dilemma included migraine headaches and a fear of driving his car, both of which seriously debilitated him. By the time the couple separated Denis finally concluded that it wasn't worth fight-ing for every hug and kiss.

While many couples are equally frustrated in similar situa-tions, some continue to live in misery for years, feeling undesirable and shut out, or harassed and bombarded. They may adjust by simply sacrificing their own needs, or they may rationalize that "things will change", or "she had a hard day." But they are not really happy.

Just as mutual interest in companionship is a crucial factor in selecting a compatible partner, mutual interest in intimacy should also be weighed carefully. The more closely your partner mirrors your personality in Talking and Touching, the more satisfactory and compatible a relationship is assured. As a closer balance is attained in both socialization and warmth, conflict is minimized and happiness becomes predictable. Danielle put it nicely: "It's like looking in a mirror, I see so much of myself in Chad. We don't agree on everything, but we're very much alike."

Each of us enters the adult world with verbal and physical needs and responses which have been learned and absorbed by observing and interacting with our family. But each of us will meet many other people who will have widely varying needs for communication based on their own individual childhood experiences. To have our own needs for Talking and Touching fulfilled, our partner must be someone with similar needs. Otherwise, both partners will be frustrated, dissatisfied and miserable, as in this story.

"When I first knew Patrick, he was a more spontaneous and outgoing person," Elayne said at the time of her first counseling session. "It seemed like one minute I was with a loving person and the next minute I was trying to figure out why he changed so much." She was a disillusioned young woman who had been married for nine years and was under a considerable amount of pressure from several upsetting events. After innumerable talks with Patrick about the gradual decrease of their intimacy, over the years she had developed interest in a co-worker who had recently separated from his wife of thirteen years. Subsequently her brother was killed in an automobile accident. After Elayne's futile attempts to talk to Patrick about the distance and isolation she continued to feel, her clandestine meetings with her co-worker increased. Justin put pressure on Elayne to see him more often, especially in the evenings. Elayne experienced sleep and weight loss. Meanwhile, she maintained her social obligations in her marriage. One day as she was having lunch with Justin at their favorite meeting place, she caught the eye of a close friend of Patrick's. Elayne returned home that night torn between guilt over her infidelity to Patrick and the frustration of repressed needs for so many years.

After a restless night, she decided to separate and move to her own apartment. She confronted Patrick as he was dressing for work the next morning. As he brushed by her in their dressing room, Elayne sensed that Patrick was "not in the mood" to discuss their marriage. Later that morning she packed an overnight bag and left, feeling totally helpless and despondent. After several months Elayne was still tormented by feelings of confusion and frustration. As Elayne continued to explore her feelings in counseling she began to gain a better understanding of her needs, and their divergent personalities. She came to terms with the fact that she had been overly dependent on her husband and that she had allowed her personality to be altered according to his moods and whims. When he wanted to talk, they talked; when he wanted to go out, they socialized, and when he wanted intimacy, they were intimate. If she proposed one of her needs, Patrick determined if he would meet it or not. As she looked at her relationship from many aspects, her determination to proceed with a divorce became evident. At the end of her therapy Elayne was close to the day of her divorce and had decided to discontinue her relationship with her co-worker. She said, "For the first time in my life I feel like my own person, not someone else's shadow."

Since relationships don't change personalities, and personalities don't change relationships, it is desirable to know yourself well before you seek your MATCH. To more readily determine your need for verbal and physical intimacy review the following lists.

LIST "A"

1. Can you comfortably show your feelings in a love relationship?
2. When you are given a compliment or gift, do you find it easy to express your appreciation?
3. Do you like to talk and freely converse about yourself?
4. Can you go into a crowd of new people and initiate conversation?
5. Can you openly show affection without feeling uncomfortable and embarrassed?

LIST "B"

1. Do your friends say you are reserved or the quiet type?
2. Do you prefer staying out of the spotlight in conversation?
3. Are you a shy person?
4. Do you have a pattern of cutting off conversations when you feel uncomfortable with the topic?

5. Are you reluctant to discuss personal matters such as sex and intimacy?

6. Do you feel you have to have time to warm up before talking to strangers?

Before rating yourself on communication, remember that although societal pressures have been greater in recent years to "let it all hang out," this all-out form of openness is not for everyone. Total openness is not the only guarantee of happiness in marriage. To a low communicator, total openness would be as oppressive as total restraint would be to a high communicator. The important thing is to be aware of your own capacity for Talking and Touching, regardless of whether it is high or low, and to assess the capacity of your potential partner correctly. Happiness lies in marrying someone with the same capacity for verbal and non-verbal communication as you have.

With this in mind, now rate yourself in communication on a scale of one to seven, with seven being the warmest and most open person, and one being a person who is reserved and cautious about showing his feelings. Enter your score in the box below.

1	2	3	4	5	6	7

Knowing your own ratings in sociability (from Chapter IV) and in communication give you one-half of the knowledge you need to select a compatible partner. The other half is the rating of any potential partner in these same areas. The person who has the same ratings as you or is within one point of you in either direction will be an ideal partner.

Remember, when you are evaluating partners, don't be fooled. Being at a party does not make someone sociable, and talking a lot does not make someone warm.

Chapter VI

Compromise: The Middle Road in Decision Making

M: mirror image: a similar personality type.

A: activity level: an equal interest in socialization.

T: talking and touching: a corresponding need for verb
non-verbal communication..

C: COMPROMISE: COOPERATIVE DECISION- MAKIN

H: harmony: mutual acceptance.

Compromise: The Middle Road in Decision Making

Let us assume you have been fortunate enough to meet someone who is physically attractive and is also your mirror image in Activity and Communication. What now? In addition to finding a companion to talk to and to go places with, people desire mates who are cooperative, sensitive and responsive to their needs, both serious and trivial. To be aware of your partners needs and he of yours is one of the keys to successful relationships. But the individual needs of two people will be different at times, and these are the times when decisions must be made which are based on compromise, a willingness to meet each other halfway. For this reason the capacity of a potential partner to engage in compromise is yet another important factor in choosing partners.

Compromise comes readily to adults who were raised in a family where everyone's needs were considered in a democratic fashion, where sharing and cooperation is a natural part of everyday life. Couples who are able to negotiate their differences and arrive at a mutually satisfactory compromise are busy talking over and resolving their differences with their mates. There are, however, two types of partners for whom the daily process of decision-making is very difficult: first, the forceful, domineering person; and second, the dependent, submissive individual. One type can make up both his and his mate's mind, the other cannot make up his mind at all.

My client, Sara, who believes in compromise, was frustrated with her husband's forceful manner. She had no desire to control or be controlled and enjoyed talking over decisions. Christopher, whose needs were, for the most part, overlooked by his parents, was raised in a "do-as-I-say-and-don't ask-questions" home and enjoys having the final say with Sara, even though he tried to soften the blow by adding, "It's for your own good." Sara seethed inside when he insisted she quit her job of eight years to stay home and raise their child. Her brown eyes brimmed with tears when she told me, "Christopher feels a woman's place is in the home. My boss and I even worked out an agreement so I could work fewer hours a week. That plan was vetoed, too. Christopher says we don't need the money and I should be happy at home. "I cry all the time, not in front of Christopher, of course, "She added. "I don't have the strength to work and fight him, too. With Christopher it's don't do this, don't do that, don't do everything. I didn't get married to be bossed around."

Friction between Christopher and Sara diminished after Christopher joined our sessions. As they discussed their disagreements, a compromise was reached. Sara continued to work part-time, and Christopher gradually came to listen to her needs. At their last meeting Sara said, "We're talking things over now more than ever. I feel more married and closer to Christopher than I've felt for a long time."

Martin married into a relationship in which Denise assumed a parental role. Compromise was impossible. "It's like being married to my mother", Martin said to me while twisting his wedding ring. Denise comments on everything I say or do. I'm terrified to make a suggestion. I feel like she's always right and I'm always wrong." During counseling Martin began to learn to speak up for his own needs more, and Denise began to relinquish her domination.

Vern has a different story to tell about his submissive wife. "When we were married Laura insisted that I decide everything; where we lived, who we socialized with and even what we had for dinner. If she ever had a need, I didn't know it. The more she clung to me, the more frustrated and angry I became. Before our separation seven months ago, she refused to leave our house to shop or attend any social events. The more I did, the less she did. It was as though she became a totally helpless person without a thought or idea of her own, a prisoner in her own home. I left before the house came down on my head."

Andrew learned early in his 12-year relationship with Christine that over the years the combination of her pushing and his backing down to avoid conflicts sabotaged their relationship. At the time Andrew and I talked, Christine had insisted that her rebellious teenage brother come to live with them. Andrew was strongly opposed to the arrangement. "I'm not backing down anymore," he said. As they talked about the conditions under which this might be workable, he and Christine decided together that her brother could live with them, providing that he could abide by Andrew's house rules. Christine agreed. She remarked that she too did not want to unconditionally assume responsibility for raising her brother. They agreed to a six-month trial to see how the boy handled a stricter lifestyle.

A cooperative interchange in decision making is out of the question if one must either second-guess or define a partner's needs. An adult without stated needs is simply cast adrift to be battered by life's whims. This kind of partner becomes caught up in what I call the Magic Mate Syndrome, a tendency to look upon one's mate as omnipotent, all-knowing. With the wave of a magic wand one's needs are automatically anticipated and met. The person with the Magic Mate Syndrome believes that he participates in a relationship, when in reality his submissive tendencies run interference with his true needs.

One young woman told of her despair as the Magic Mate to her husband of two years. "If only I knew what he wanted, I would be happy," Angela said. "What can you do with someone who says, 'I don't know' or I don't care' to every suggestion?

"We're married. He should know what I want," a husband or wife may state emphatically. But needs change from day to day and hour to hour. How can someone, however intimate, anticipate the immediate need of another person at all times? Marriage is not a mind-reading game where decisions can be reached on the basis of one partner guessing what the other desires. This creates an imbalance in the decision-making process.

The most straightforward way to negotiate needs in a relationship consists of three steps:

1. Each partner must identify his own needs.

2. Each partner must make his needs known to his mate.

3. Both partners must strive for a compromise which considers the needs of both parties.

This process is vastly better than doggedly concealing your needs while your frustrated partner tries to second-guess them, or heavily handedly forcing your own needs upon your partner. The essence of compromise lies in meeting each other halfway. This process is stymied by both the domineering partner who must have the whole road to himself and the submissive partner who simply won't travel the road at all. Since not a day goes by when some decision must be made by marriage partners, the need for constant interchange is essential to a long and happy union. Moreover, exchanging needs is a necessary form of verbal intimacy which is enhanced during the process of reaching a compromise together.

However, the manner in which two people make decisions during courtship, an unusually accommodating period of time, can be drastically affected by marriage As one newlywed complained to me: "I believed my husband liked to dance because we decided to go dancing every weekend when we were dating. Marriage seems to have changed all that. He never takes me dancing anymore and the subject has never come up since."

Evan and Charlene had been married for two years when they made their first appointment with me. They felt at odds with each other over most decisions. For example, Evan wanted to buy a house with a large mortgage, while Charlene wanted to stay in their apartment until they had saved a sizeable down payment. Several weeks of heated meetings passed before they were able to consider the merits of a compromise. A noticeably deeper intimacy between Evan and Charlene resulted from this new found capacity for compromise. How did they solve their problem? They decided to live in an apartment long enough to save a minimum down payment for a house.

One of the major sources of friction and frustration between partners, which frequently leads to a need for counseling, occurs when one partner halfheartedly agrees to meet the needs of the other without seriously weighing his own needs. This results in either a barrage of complaints from the "agreeable" partner or a pointed display of pouting and sullenness.

At many a party a reluctant socializer can be found hovering in a quiet corner, longing for his favorite hearth side chair, while across the room his partner is pleasurably engaged in a lively group conversation. One scenario begins with the ride home; so do the recriminations: "Whose idea was it to go to <u>that</u> party?" . . "I didn't talk to one interesting person all evening." . . . "Whatever happened to the good old days when families stayed home and entertained themselves?" And later, in the quiet of the bedroom, the wife sighs into her pillow: "I knew I should have gone alone to that party. He won't speak to me for a week! Why didn't he just say he didn't want to go?" Why don't partners state their needs and feelings; work the decision through, without contradicting his own needs and then punishing his partner with sullen silence? For those who lack self confidence, negotiating one's needs are difficult. When decisions are not made with consideration for both partners' needs, the relationship is jeopardized in several critical ways. The spirit of a cooperative partnership is undermined, causing the relationship to erode. Mates become adversaries. Unable to arrive at a middle-of-the-ground solution, communication breaks down in other areas of daily life. Negative feelings grow and lie seething just below the surface until each party's true needs are re-negotiated and solved. This process may take hours, days, weeks, months or even years.

For Allison and Lyle, a compromise was delayed for six years. They began their annual feud every August, one month before deer season opened. Coincidentally their wedding anniversary occurred during deer season, and each year Lyle and three business buddies went off to the mountains to hunt while Allison stayed home alone. When they tried to talk it over in counseling, Lyle ended each discussion with, "I warned you before we married that I never miss deer season." Allison was left feeling defeated and depressed. "We've stopped being intimate and we don't go out. We're both thinking about divorce," she told me. "Can you help us?" Allison and I talked about several compromises which might work. She later told me, "Lyle and I stayed up one night until 5 a.m., and we really talked for the first time in months, each listening to the other." For six years we've never celebrated our anniversary together, she hesitantly told him. Lyle responded: "I didn't know that celebrating our anniversary meant that much to you. After six years of marriage you would think I could pick up on these things. But you never said anything, so I thought you liked the time alone," he continued. They talked over their options. The decision they made in the early morning dawn was to plan an anniversary trip of their own the weekend before deer season opened. To couples who are readily able to compromise and meet each other halfway, Allison and Lyle's situation may seem ludicrous. But anyone who has succumbed to a half-hearted decision out of fear of naming his needs or to keep the risk of rejection or negative response to a minimum can understand that Allison's departure from her usual submissive behavior required courage. There are multitudes of submissive people like Allison who find life a constant uphill battle to have their needs met.

Short delays in coming to an agreeable compromise are perfectly normal. But too many half-hearted decisions lead to extended family feuds, inflicting temporary and sometimes permanent damage to a relationship.

The signs are quite familiar: days or weeks without exchanging a word, one partner sleeping on the living room couch, an empty chair at the family dinner table, slammed doors and broken dishes. Cold wars and heated arguments are deeply disrupting forces which immobilize a couple's relationship and place a strain on the best of relationships. During the whole period when partners drag along halfheartedly, their relationship remains inert. They are aware of being at odds, but unaware of how to break the stalemate. Negotiation and compromise are the keys to avoid these grim detours which lead nowhere. Each partner must be willing to share his actual needs and to listen to the needs of the other one. Then a decision which encompasses those mutual needs must be reached, a decision which represents a mutually satisfactory compromise between a domineering "we'll-do-it-my-way" and a submissive "we'll-do-it-your-way." Compromise requires the candor and cooperation of both partners, but it is richly rewarded when a decision is negotiated which truly reflects: "We'll-do-it-our-way."

Negotiating has the added benefit of bringing about greater sensitivity in partners, as one's own needs are shared and as one attempts to listen to and respond to the needs of the other party. Somewhere between the Magic Mate and a controlled parent-child relationship lies the middle road of Compromise where cooperative partners can travel along in a mature give-and-take relationship.

In seeking a mate with whom you will be sharing decisions for a lifetime, you should carefully weigh the answers to these questions about any potential partners.

1. Is he unyielding when he makes up his mind?

2. Does he believe in peace at any price?

3. Does he disagree just to disagree?

4. Does he push for a need and then pull back?

Marriage will not change your answers to any of these questions. If anything, conflicts will intensify and be magnified as time passes.

A successful marriage is the result of two cooperative partners negotiating and compromising their way through life's many decisions. If love conquers all, it is precisely because love is able to Compromise!

Chapter VII

Harmony: Mutual Acceptance

M: mirror image: a similar personality type.

A: activity level: an equal interest in socialization.

T: talking and touching: a corresponding need for verb non-verbal communication.

C: compromise: cooperative decision- making.

H: HARMONY: MUTUAL ACCEPTANCE.

Harmony: Mutual Acceptance

"Do you take this person for better or for worse, for richer or for poorer, in sickness and in health. . ."

If you are thinking that the meaning of those marriage vows is that you will want mutual acceptance for the rest of your life, you are right. The words express their message quite clearly: the two partners must accept each other as they really are, regardless of circumstances, for the rest of their lives. Loving someone as he really is, with no compelling need to change his manners, his habits, his personality, is true compatibility. Acceptance does not lay blame for overdrawing the checking account or criticize your appearance or personality. All the more reason to make sure that you not only love, but like the type of partner you are about to choose. Mutual patience and understanding, between partners who genuinely like each other as they are, in addition to loving each other, creates harmonious lifestyles.

Courtship is a time when each partner shows his best side and sees only the best side of the other. Conversation is scintillating, decorum is flawless, and decisions are mutual. Marriage seems to change these ground rules. In a sudden turnabout some partners become antagonistic, critical and hostile. How does this happen?

As we have seen in the previous chapters, many personality characteristics are acquired from our parents. Children who were reared in an atmosphere of constant criticism tend to grow up to find fault with those around them, most notable with the perfect built-in victim, the husband or wife. These people project onto their mates verbal and sometimes physical injury which generates disharmony in their lives. During the dating period these destructive tendencies go into remission, only to become painfully evident after marriage.

After three years of marriage Francine summarized for me her reaction to Sean's hostility toward her: "He's like the judge and jury. Whether I'm cooking a meal, making a bed or talking on the phone, he's right there ready to critique everything I do. I can never be myself."

We all want to be liked and accepted by our partners just as we are, but how many of us give careful consideration before marriage to whether our potential partner is the type of personality who will be able to accept us non-critically and with patience?

Disguised hostility before marriage is common. In the vernacular this is called putting your best foot forward. After marriage, behavior reverts to natural tendencies. The date who once impatiently darted in and out of traffic is now impatiently demanding that the lawn be mowed. The date who once criticized a football player's error is now criticizing his spouse's attire, bookkeeping, table manners and laundry detergent. It cannot be reiterated often enough that people do not change after marriage. They simply relax and become their everyday selves. The best foot, which has been forward during courtship, slips backward, and acquired personality characteristics take over, to a greater extent than we are fully aware.

My client, Wally describes his experiences with his outspoken wife after four years of marriage: "Janelle was always doing things to get even with people, and that always bothered me. We hadn't been married three months when she began to alienate every member of my family. Even when we were dating she always had a chip on her shoulder. She says she only tells it like it is and I'm too sensitive. I've tried everything to get her to change: I agree, disagree, keep quiet, stay out of the way. Nothing works."

To wait for a partner to move out of his self-created war zone is agonizing. What does one do when he finds himself face-to face with the reality that his mate is argumentative, shutting out others one by one? First, your partner is not speaking to your mother, then her sister, then your father, then the neighbors. Before long you get the feeling you may be next. My client, Joshua, explained, "Sometimes I feel that Gina is playing Ten Little Indians, and soon there will be none. I am the only one she talks to anymore, and I do not know how long that will last."

Sometimes a partner's change in attitude may be subtle and appear unexpectedly on the scene when his confidence is at a low point. The catalyst for such a change may be anything from a death in the family to a job loss or health problems. With a drop in self-confidence comes a period of depression and a shift in tolerance. Reactions vary, sometimes bringing personality changes gradually and sometimes suddenly.

My client, Deena, noticed a big difference in Nick's personality after his firm promoted his best friend. "Our whole life seemed to be thrown out of kilter. Nick was nice one day and sarcastic and ill-tempered the next. This went on for seven months. Just when I believed our marriage was on the rocks, Nick started to act nicer."

A hostile person can unconsciously seek a mate who is exceptionally tolerant. Thus the tolerant partner becomes an easy target for the constant criticism and blame vented upon him by the hostile partner. An adult who was reared by tolerant parents is more likely to be tolerant himself, and he is also more likely to believe others are similarly tolerant. Unfortunately, dating does not always reveal the full extent of a potential partner's hostile tendencies. Even more unfortunately, marriage is the fertile field in which hostility can be brought to full fruition, with heart breaking consequences.

Amy, a recent bride, came to talk with me about her anxiety toward her husband: "It's not bad enough that every night Kent comes home from work and drinks himself into a stupor. Lately he's begun to blame me for everything that goes wrong. It's my fault he didn't get his long awaited raise. It's my fault he and his new boss don't see eye to eye. It's even my fault we don't get along anymore. And to top it off, I'm driving him to drink!"

Hostility in marriage takes many traditional forms: grudge-holding - "If you'd gotten that promotion three years ago, we'd be driving a BMW now instead of a Volkswagen bus"; Fault-finding - "Why are you vacuuming now?"; The Hyper-Critic - "You hung that picture an inch too high"; and the Silent Treatment, for which no quote is available. Add to this list the usual daily misunderstandings, oversights and tactless remarks and you have fuel enough for a continuous series of hot or cold wars between spouses.

To discover after marriage that the agreeable person you remember from dating days has been transformed into a contentious adversary is a devastating experience. This is exactly what happened to Juliette: "After we were married, Lance became a constant reminder that I couldn't do anything right. I couldn't cook like a chef or make a bed like an Army officer. It doesn't seem fair. My Dad always picked on my Mom the way Lance picks on me. I feel like I'm being constantly punished."

Juliette's appraisal of her dilemma is correct. She is indeed being asked, not at all politely, to change, to conform to Lance's desired image of her, to be what he wants her to be. Lance is hostile and he cannot accept Juliette *as she is*; he does not approve of the type of person she is. Lance may love Juliette in his own way, but he does not like her. So Lance picks on Juliette to vent his hostility toward her and to change her to meet his standards.

In any sound partnership each person should feel secure and comfortable with the other. This is only possible if two people are not antagonistic and critical toward each other. Mutual acceptance brings harmony to a marriage, while hostility breeds havoc.

To choose a marriage partner is not like choosing a fine suit, where you accept the product after it has been altered to your personal specifications. Partners come already custom made, and it is the prime responsibility of two potential mates to assess carefully each other's particular specifications to determine whether they are mutually suited to each other. Otherwise, to continue the analogy, an ill-fitting marriage will result in a marriage in which neither partner is comfortable or happy.

No two partners this side of sainthood live in perfect peace day in and day out. But two people whose personalities are compatible are able to achieve this harmony because neither partner wishes to change the other.

Marriage tends to foster the notion that a person can get used to anything, but this is not so. Relationships in which a person is nagged, criticized, judged or condemned by the person who vowed to love them "until death do us part" soon becomes strained. My client, Caroline's, problem was typical: "He killed any feeling I had for him. First the verbal outbursts, and then the pushing around. The day my husband shoved me against our living room wall and said, 'You do what I say or else,' I realized things weren't going to change, not after six years. I walked! We didn't have much in common, anyway."

Marriage should be a sanctuary from the turmoil of daily life, not a source of even greater turmoil. To insure a harmonious marriage, a marriage in which you can be loved for yourself, read over the following checklist of questions to ask yourself about any potential partners.

1. Is he quick to forgive and forget?

2. Is he argumentative, quick-tempered or sarcastic?

3. Does he find it difficult to accept criticism?

4. Does he apologize readily when wrong?

5. Does he bear grudges?

6. Does he feel everyone is entitled to a second chance?

7. Is he critical and impatient with others?

8. Is he tactful in his dealings with others?

If you answered "yes" to number one, four, six and eight, then your potential partner will be able to accept you as you are. If you answered "yes" to numbers two, three, five and seven, your potential partner is more likely to manifest hostility, attempting through criticism and other negative behavior to change you to suit himself.

Approaching marriage as a serious, life-long relationship should encourage us to be as logical and rational as possible in choosing a partner. Too often we judge only the superficial qualities of a potential mate, overlooking the submerged personality traits which will surface later. We have all met hostile people who are nevertheless married to devoted spouses. But constantly seeking the approval of your partner, forever trying to change and adjust to the criticisms and demands of your hostile mate makes for hard times. You are more likely to become aware of your partner's liking and loving ways after you tie the knot unless you accurately read the person from inside-out rather than outside-in. The best way to have acceptance is to marry into it.

Let's review for a moment the entire MATCH System which we have discussed in the preceding chapters, since positive responses to each of these areas would add up to a comfortable relationship:

1. Are you physically attracted to your potential partner?

2. Do you think that you and your potential partner are mirror Images of each other's personalities?

3. Do you and your potential partner share the same Activity Level, move at the same social pace?

4. Do you and your potential partner share a desire for the same degree of Talking and Touching?

5. Do you and your potential partner arrive at decisions through negotiation and cooperation?

6. Are you mutually accepting?

No miracle after marriage is going to transform Mr. or Mrs. Wrong into a compatible lifetime partner. It is far easier and more intelligent to assess a potential mate rationally before marriage than to become a painful casualty of mismatching on a battlefield of conflict.

Chapter VIII

Fighting The Odds With a Near Match or Mismatch

Many say they dislike gambling, but in each divorce is a gambler who was fighting the odds when he chose a near match or mismatch for a partner. There are those couples who match and marry. What were their guidelines for a successful choice -- more than likely they just got lucky! If in the passion of love, or in the name of love, you are thinking of choosing a partner in whom you are willing to take a chance on love alone, the stakes are high. You can change your place of residency, your job or partners, but you cannot change types of personality--once married.

The three avenues in which people are most likely to sabotage their chances for a successful choice of mates is to confuse sociability with warmth, love with passion and emotion with logic.

Some give you a reason, some never try, but behind every divorce is a person who really believed that their expectations about marriage would be filled. My clients tell it this way. Only later does it become clear that once mismatched, they were fighting the odds while waiting for changes to come about. None came! Bewilderment and disbelief. It couldn't happen to me! Then frustration and anger. First fighting and then making up. Later the excitement of living with an opposite type begins to wear thin. Expectations dim and, last but not least, where there used to be love now he feels indifferent. Maybe it was easy to shut their eyes while dating; now the reality sets in while they emotionally check out. Why did it happen to me he asks himself. Marriage works for others, then it should work for me!

The reasons people have given me for staying in relationships which are not compatible are:

I don't believe in divorce.

I feel guilty about leaving my partner.

I feel sorry for my partner.

I'm staying married until the children are raised.

I hope things will improve.

I have financial security.

I've learned to be patient and overlook a lot.

I'm determined to make this marriage work.

I've invested too much in this relationship to give up.

I'm afraid to be alone.

I believe my partner will change in time.

I don't want to feel like a failure.

None of these reasons inspire hope for a better tomorrow. Marriage should be a source of happiness, comfort, consolation and deep satisfaction. In past chapters we have covered the five important steps of the MATCH System which, if followed, will assist a person in choosing a compatible partner as well as in avoiding a destructive choice. These various elements of the MATCH System included:

M Mirror Image: a person similar to me in personality.

A Activity Level: a person who likes to socialize outside the home as much or as little as I do.

T Talking and Touching: a person whose need for verbal and physical communication is the same as mine.

C Cooperation: a person who is able to express his needs, listens to my needs and negotiate a mutually agreeable compromise.

H Harmony: a person who can accept me for who I am.

You will recall that in two of these areas, Activity Level and Talking and Touching (communication), you scored yourself on a scale of one to seven. A "one" in Activity would represent a person who would not choose to participate in any away-from-home activity more than one night a week, whereas a "five" would be willing to go out regularly five nights a week to eat, see a movie, bowl or attend meetings. A "one" in Talking and Touching would represent a person who was very reserved and inward, expressed his feelings very sparingly, and probably will not engage in much touching or hugging, whereas a "five" or "six" would be likely to share most of his innermost feelings and express his affection with a great deal of physical contact. As we discussed, the important point in rating yourself is not how high or low you might score, but that this score gives you the self-knowledge you need to choose a compatible partner. People come in many varieties; they can be socially involved and participate in a myriad of activities, and yet be reserved and cautious about sharing their inner feelings and details about their lives. Likewise, there are those who enjoy talking and touching; warm homebodies who dislike being on the go.

In scoring a potential partner in these two crucial areas of Activity and Talking and Touching, you will find one of three possibilities:

1. A good match: the same scores or a one-point difference (for example: 3/3 or 4/5).

2. A near match scores with a two-point difference (for example 4/6 or 1/3).

3. A mismatch: scores with a difference of three or more points (for example: 1/4 or 3/7).

The first step is to know yourself. What type of personality are you? How would you rate your own sociability? To what degree do you enjoy talking and touching? Are you able to listen to another persons' needs and, knowing your own needs, arrive at a reasonable compromise? Are you an accepting person? Self-knowledge provides you with a healthy head start in choosing a compatible partner.

So much for your side of the equation. In order to balance it with the proper partner you must spend some time getting to know the other person. The first prerequisite of any lasting marital relationship is physical attraction. Let's presume you meet someone you find physically attractive. Now the question to be answered is, "how can you tell if you have found your match?" You cannot by first looking! It is more a matter of *asking* what you need to know and *listening* to what each person reveals about himself in order to decide if it is wise to continue the relationship. If you know your ratings on sociability and communication, you will know the type who meets your needs. Now the challenge begins.

The person you just met looks and acts just so; he is nice enough to say "hello", friendly enough to put you at ease, attractive enough to make your heart skip a beat; and encouraging enough to make you feel hopeful that at last you found Mr. or Miss Wonderful. Is it a match of mismatch? Is his Activity Level the same as or within one point of yours? Once again, that is a question which easily could be asked between the main course and dessert. Remember in future dating to re-evaluate you partner's score. Dating is a time when two people are trying hard to make a good impression on each other. It is also a time when two people go out to socialize a lot more than they usually do. Remember that a person's Activity Level is measured by the number of nights of each week he is willing to spend regularly away from home, whether alone or in the company of his spouse or friends. If you know that you are a "two and your potential partner seems to be a "one", "two or "three", then compatibility is possible with this person. If, however, your "two" decides to pair up with a "four, "five", "six" or "seven" you are running the risk of a serious mismatch in social activity. Your inclination to stay home and your partner's inclination to go out will be a source on ongoing conflict and stress in your marital relationship.

Talking and Touching is the second area where observation of your potential partner is important to avoid a disastrous mismatch. Let's say that you scored yourself a "three" for Talking and Touching, which would make you a modestly conversational and affectionate person who would find a good match in another "two, "three or "four. But were your "three to vow a lifetime in the company of a "five, "six or "seven", your married life would be difficult, even impossible. Should you escape being overwhelmed by the constant verbal expressiveness of your mate, you would have to cope with your guilt at being unable to respond to his physical demonstrativeness. Your partner, conversely would feel rejected in both of these areas.

Dating is a time when most decisions are made with mutual thoughtfulness, each party trying to please the other. As you and your potential mate come to know each other better, you should know how decisions are being made. Does he make them all? Does he shunt all the decisions off on you? Or, ideally, do you both state your needs and cooperate in arriving at an agreeable compromise?

Harmony is the final area to observe your potential partner before marriage. Can he accept you as you are, personality intact, blemishes included? Is it all right with this person that you laugh too loud, slurp your soup, read science fiction and like classical music? Or will this person set about teaching you social graces, table manners, reading habits and new musical taste? In other words, does he like you enough to let you be yourself? Or does his hostility force him to nag and criticize you into becoming the person he wants you to be?

The better you match your potential partner, the better the marriage. The more opposite you are, the more difficult the marriage. In the areas of Activity Level (social) and Talking and Touching (communication), it is important that you and your potential partner are either the same score or within one point of each other (good match). Two points apart in these two crucial areas indicates a mismatch. Three or more points apart promise hard times for both partners in a marriage that will almost inevitably end in divorce.

No one marries to be unhappy. When bride and groom exchage vows, it is with the full expectation that their marriage will be solid, loving and happy. Yet one-half of all marriages end in divorce. Fifty percent of the couples who pledge to love, honor and obey end up at some point bewildered, frustrated and angry that their marriage could end in failure, that love could give way to indifference. How could this happen?

I firmly believe marriages which end in divorce do so because the two partners were mismatched in the first place. In other words, their marriage was doomed from the start. They may have had some misgivings about their future partner before marrying, but they glossed over their doubts both before and during their marriage with various rationales:

> Life will be more exciting and challenging with an opposite personality.
>
> I'll teach my partner to be more sociable, loving, cooperative and patient in time.
>
> In time we'll get used to each other's ways.
>
> If I hold on a little longer, he/she will change.
>
> He/she will learn to accept me the way I am.

Closing your eyes to the signs of incompatibility before marriage, thinking that love can conquer personality differences, hoping that time will solve the problems that you can't solve, are all ways of dodging the hard truth: that you and your partner may be mismatched. How much more intelligent it is to approach a potential partner with a strong sense of your own needs and some solid criteria for judging his capacity as a lifetime mate.

Does timing make a difference? Yes. Sometimes a person can meet the perfect partner at the wrong time. One astute client, Pam, said to me: "I just got out of one relationship, and I'm afraid I'll get hurt again. This new person and I are a lot alike, but I wish I'd met him before I was married and divorced."

Likewise, rebound relationships can occur at a time when a lack of self-confidence makes logical and realistic decisions about partner selection very difficult.

Evonn, a waitress, who remarried after a ten month divorce, talks about her experience: "I don't think I gave myself enough time. I don't know what I was trying to prove after my husband left me for a younger woman. I guess I thought we would be even once I remarried, too. It isn't fair to my husband."

Tad, divorced for four years, reports that he will never again put himself in the position of making a commitment. After Coleen, his wife of five years, left with his two children, he began to work long hours at the office and to restrict his social life to an occasional movie and dinner with a variety of women. "I don't have time for a steady relationship," he says. "Maybe it's an ego problem, but I was stunned when Coleen left. We got along just fine when we were married. They say time heals everything, but I wonder!" I don't think I'll ever get seriously involved with another woman again."

Periods of situational depressions, when a person "isn't himself" can lend confusion in choosing a mate. Monica was in her senior year in college, majoring in journalism and active in her sorority, when she was called home. Her father had been hospitalized after a heart attack. Back on campus and after weeks of anxiety about her father's health, she began to withdraw. She declined her nomination for sorority president the following year. Warren met Monica at a fraternity party that her roommate had coaxed her into attending. After five months of quiet library and coffee dates, he and Monica were pinned and planned to marry after graduation in June. Her dad had recovered and was able to give the bride away.

As Monica's depression lifted, her need for activity increased. As she tried to involve Warren in more social outings, he resisted, saying, "I don't mind socializing, but I don't want it to be a major part of our lives." Timing! As Warren and Monica discovered, its not easy to recognize true personality traits when one "isn't himself."

Since neither a person on the rebound, or someone in a depressed state will project a true picture of his personality, it is very difficult to accurately read the signs of compatibility at these times.

Should you choose to marry a mismatch, you will have to work hard to conquer the odds. There is little promise of success. Tara was in her early thirties and had been married for four years at the time of our first session. She was concerned because, like her parents, she found herself struggling to keep her marriage together. She knew that she was more outgoing than Daniel and that her friends sought her out,, only to be put off by Daniel. She couldn't figure out why he was so miserable, especially when she entertained at home. It became clear to Tara rather quickly that Daniel resented the privacy of his home being invaded by anyone, including neighbors, friends and Tara's family. Communication between Tara and Daniel at this point was limited to polite conversation.

Tara did not want her marriage to end in divorce, however, over the months Tara's frustration increased. First, she planned her social activities away from home. Then she tried to be away only during the times that Daniel was also gone. Finally Tara realized that "Daniel cannot accept me or my friends. If I'm going to do everything alone, I might as well be single. I don't want to give up being myself just to stay married. Now I can go out, see people and enjoy myself."

Tara, like many others, came to see that the union of extreme opposites in sociability and communication is like running an obstacle course. Mismatches are the proverbial twain which shall never meet.

How about near matches? There is more hope here. Darrin, thirty-one years old, had been married five-and-a-half years when we spoke. He said he loved his wife, Ellen, but found it difficult to supply all the warmth in their relationship. "I have a lot of love to give, and I want to share it with my wife. But Ellen comes from a family that doesn't show as much affection as mine. She's a good listener though." Darrin and Ellen enjoyed an active social life. "She's my best friend and we have fun going places together. It's just that Ellen doesn't always share her feelings with me."

With counseling, Ellen decided it was all right to let more of her feelings be known, and each of our meetings became a time to open more doors that Darrin believed were closed to him forever. These near matches worked their problem through to a happy conclusion.

Other near matches find themselves in a situation like Vince and Brittany, who came to counseling after six-and-a-half years of a wonderful marriage, full of intimacy and closeness. He spoke openly about Brittany's frustration and resentment with their social life. She was equally candid. Vince is a homebody, but Brittany would like to have three or four outside activities a week planned with him. Why is this so difficult? He said, "I could go out every time she wants me to but if I go I'm miserable." "I feel guilty leaving Vince home", Brittany said. Ultimately they made a compromise. Since Vince didn't mind being out once a week, he agreed that Brittany should pursue one of her hobbies away from home on two other nights. As Vince came to accept Brittany's desire to be out a little more than he was, he looked forward to taking her out, and she began to enjoy both her evening out with Vince and the freedom to attend her exercise classes without Vince's disapproval.

Near matches are able to work out their differences by bringing their needs out into the open and negotiating a mutually agreeable compromisc. Unfortunatcly, couples who are as dissimilar as Tara and Daniel, who are definitely mismatched, are not usually able to negotiate their differences, since they are starting from so much farther apart. Regardless of their attempts to fall in step with each other's needs, their lives remain off balance. Marriage becomes a battleground. The power struggle to remain oneself while married to an opposite overshadows the relationship, good intentions notwithstanding.

Marriage is a partnership which is highly sensitive to extreme dissimilarities that affect companionship and communication. Think of the mate selection like a dart game, where you may choose your match (right on target), or a mismatch (way off target). Why not go for the bullseye and win the game!

Chapter IX

What To Do If . . .

What would you do if your partner tells you:

- He wants a divorce after one year of marriage.
- You just don't understand me.
- I'm bored. We're home a lot.
- I f you didn't like me the way I am, why did you marry me to begin with?
- I thought we had a lot in common and now we're like two strangers living in the same house.
- You haven't made love to me in weeks.
- I can't believe it, but you'd rather read a book than talk to me.

• I need a little time away from you to find myself.

Distress Signals! That first feeling may be hurt, anger, shock, disappointment, fear or helplessness. But what do you do? Try harder? Give up? Give in? Look for professional help? Will you stay married? Separate? Divorce?

How you react at this time is critical. Do you strike back? Try to get even? Retreat and hope the problem will disappear? You can look to friends, neighbors or family members to tell you what they would do . . . but do not refuse to acknowledge legitimate complaints from your partner. It's the long way around. Individuals will disguise their true needs for a time, but will bring them forth, either directly or indirectly, as their frustrations build.

It's rare to marry and live together "forever" without undergoing a certain amount of stress. At the time of the first distress signal:

... Take a simple direct approach ask your partner what is the *exact* source of stress.

... Be alert to periods of unusually high stress for your mate as: the busy season at work and deadlines for certain projects.

... Be more cautious when the complaints center around either your social life or verbal and non-verbal communication.

... Remember that the odds are on your side if you are compatible in sociability and communication.

In order to develop sufficient insight and more tolerance before you draw a conclusion ask yourself these questions:

1. Do your opposing needs reflect conflict from stressful situations rather than personality differences?

2. Is the change in your partner's behavior mostly directed toward pressure outside the relationship rather than toward you?

3. Are you reacting to stress as though your relationship is in jeopardy rather than waiting for outside pressure on your partner to lessen?

4. If the issue reflects differences in your personalities, are you feeling threatened and fearful rather than looking at both sides while carefully studying each of your needs as you keep in mind both of your actual personality traits?

5. If changes can be brought about, do they realistically reflect your needs and personalities?

If you answered "yes" to questions 1, 2 and 3, release yourself from the conflict and allow your partner to resolve his own needs. It may take hours, days or weeks for your mate to make a decision depending on the depth of his inner struggle.

Emily and Matthew were married 13 years at the time of counseling. She was highly disciplined and decisive and prides herself on her ability to make quick decisions. Matthew is slow to make changes and decisions. To Emily, Matthew's inability to decide if he should leave the family business and go into business for himself is intolerable. Matthew dreads going out on his own. To him, the family business gives him a sense of direction and security which he does not want to relinquish. On the other hand, daily bouts with his uncle who is president of the company makes him anxious. Although Matthew feels that he is the type who easily gets along with others, he senses that he is regarded like a child by his uncle who is antagonistic and resistive to Matthew's new ideas even if they are in the interest of the company.

Emily said that Matthew was constantly upset at the end of the day, criticizing either her or their two children. "Our social life is nonexistent and our sex life deplorable." At the point Emily felt that Matthew's job rather than their marriage was the real issue, she became more understanding and patient. Soon after starting counseling Emily and Matthew made the necessary changes in both their social and sex life while Matthew looked for solutions about his career.

Once outside pressures enter the picture it is normal to feel threatened and fearful that these seemingly insurmountable problems will stifle your personal relationship. At this time, conflicts, changes in behavior or a breakdown in verbal and physical communication is to be expected, but need not be a sign that you are out of love, or on your way to separation or divorce.

If you concluded from items 4, and 5 that personality clashes possibly exist between you and your partner, here are some basic considerations:

Do you feel that the true source of your unhappiness is differences in either sociability or communication? In other words, are you both happy with the quality of your companionship and talking and touching in your partnership?

At first, there may be a tendency to blame superficial or circumstantial causes for your conflict rather than come face to face with the possibility of incompatibility -- legally defined as irreconcilable differences!

How can you explain the emergence of irreconcilable differences? By the conscious or unconscious conviction that people are capable of changing their personality types after marriage -- the Grand Illusion of mate selection!

As painful as it may seem, it may be necessary to look beyond time schedules, jobs, children, money and in-laws to get to the bottom of an unhappy relationship. When differences show up - and show up they will - search for the true source of your problems.

With a near-match, you can formulate compromise in the manner in which you approach socializing and communication. But what do you do when you discover you and your partner seem to have "nothing in common" -- a mismatch -- a homebody with a high energizer and a talker and a toucher with a reserved uncommunicative person? Then with serious consideration you may want to review your past and present attraction to opposites. Why is it, for example:

... you have a pattern of choosing psychological opposites?

... your relationships end in total frustration for you and your partner?

... you feel better when interacting with your same personality type?

In the words of one insightful young man, Clint, married two years, "I don't want to try anymore. Why don't people just marry the person who matches them to begin with? Otherwise, it's like hitting your head against a brick wall."

No fault marriages, like no fault divorces, start when the blaming stops. Then and only then can one come face to face with the reality that the relationship has to be compatible in order for it to endure for a lifetime. Understanding this, it will be possible to let go of the relationship and move on guilt-free.

For those striving for compromise, if you find that your enthusiasm for social activity is not on the same level or you have slowed down to meet your partner's needs; consider the following:

1. Put a social activity calendar on display where you and your partner can both see it.

2. Indicate on the top of the calendar your "A Scores (activity level) beside your names. For example Tami A = 3, Guy A = 5.

3. Mark down each social activity you anticipate participating in away from home. For example, Wednesday; I - independent time; bowling league. Friday; C = couple time: dinner and dancing. Saturday; F = family time; wedding.

4. Maintain a balance between couple, family and independent activities. For example, two mates with a three rating in activity can meet their social needs with one activity in each category per week (one couple, on family and one independent).

5. When you are told by your partner "we need to spend more time together", calculate the number of social activities that you have been devoting to couple time. A *minimum* of one couple activity *each week* is important to maintain companionship. Should this be a two hour lunch, a half hour coffee break or a movie, it's a vital after marriage "date".

6. When your partner says: "I never have a minute to myself", "I need more time alone", consider if your social calendar includes enough independent activities.

You will be able to improve the quality of your time spent together as a couple as more "me" time is developed.

7. When your partner says: "You need to spend more time with the family and less time working", check your social calendar for a greater balance in family time.

8. Give yourself a social checkup every three months. More separations and divorces follow periods of time in which social distress signals are ignored by both men and women. Many clients have said that they wish they could have had a second chance to work out social conflicts with their former mates before they drifted farther and farther apart. Many say: "If I knew it was that important, I would have gone out more with my spouse, or family or given him/her more space." For your social review, discuss your needs in terms of:

   ... do you go out alone or get together with other couples on a regular basis?

   ... do you take time out for your own activities?

   ... if you have children, do you regularly plan family activites?

9. Talk about your needs for socialization. Things can change if the couple acknowledges that the two individuals go at a different pace. You can begin to work out a variety of compromises in which both people can maintain their own style of socializing without excluding his partner or forcing activity on each other.

10. Pay close attention to signals that relate to your social life as: "We haven't been dancing, out to the movies, on a ride for a long time", "We should get together with our family more often", "I haven't had a moment to myself for six months". Tally your activities at the end

of each week and plan ahead for the next, keeping each other's "A" (Activity Level) rating in mind.

11. If you and your mate agree that the person who has the higher social rating, can plan additional independent activities, you will experience greater personal freedom and increase your chances of permanence. For example, if one partner rates 4 in activity and the other rates 2, the partner with the higher score may follow a social pattern as 1 - couple activity, 1 - family activity, 2 - independent activities, while the partner with a 2 rating maintains 1 - couple and 1 - family activity. Other compromises: Occasionally the individual with the lower rating (2) can add an additional activity to his schedule: (example: 1 - family, 1 - couple and 1 - independent).

If you are a one in social and your partner is a "hermit" and does not agree to go out one time a week, extend an invitation to join you in an outing. If he/she declines your suggestion for couple time, plan an independent activity or a family activity. Don't forfeit your need to socialize once a week.

If you feel that the two of you are unable to agree on the importance of change or to set new goals for socialization, seek professional help.

To marry and only then to discover that you and your mate are one of a kind in communication . . . one listener and one talker, can be a startling revelation. Since communication is not only necessary for decision making and problem solving, but the avenue for maintaining verbal and physical intimacy, conflicts in this area can be critical. If even at first you refuse to acknowledge, if only to yourself, that there is a communication gap between you and your partner, differences will soon become a reality. The very intimate nature of marriage can soon intensify the fear of the lower communicator to become involved physically or verbally or the higher communicator to become stifled.

Since most of us are unable to see ourselves as a person who holds back feelings or acts reserved, your mate is more likely to notice changes. For the lower communicator who does not share the higher needs of his mate for talking and touching, it is normal to feel overexposed to his partner's attempts for verbal and physical intimacy.

Likewise it is difficult for a spontaneous partner to be understanding when he is met by resistance for being open and responsive. For people who grew up in homes where a show of affection was an every day occurrence it is not easy to stifle or subdue their natural warmth. Once he finds himself married to a lower communicator, it may be disconcerting to discover that a partner who was responsive while dating, becomes unresponsive or openly critical of his mate's affectionate ways.

For the talker, communication comes naturally and spontaneously; for the listener, his nature is to be reserved and to enjoy periods of silence. To understand this much and to accept each other's reactions, we do not have to vow to get the higher communicator to talk or touch less or the lower communicator to talk or touch more: all that is needed is to mutually agree that each person's approach to communication is different. Do not allow feelings of rejection or disapproval to interfere with the quality of your communication. Work toward mutual communication goals.

The marriage everybody wants is the one you believed in the day you married - the one in which you both will be able to sustain feelings of sharing and caring. But what do you do when your partner says: "We don't talk like we used to", "he/she does all the talking", all we discuss is money, kids and chores around the house", "everytime we try to talk, we argue."

How do you keep the lines of communication open? First acknowledge that the higher and lower communicators have different needs. Talk about your individual needs for verbal and physical intimacy. Set aside a minimum of 10-15 minutes at the beginning and end of each day for sharing non-sexual verbal and physical intimacy in a place without distractions or interruptions. Reserve this time for non-household business and decision making.

When your "other half" likes to listen more than talk:

... show more interest in the things that interest your mate.

... acknowledge that talking all the time is not necessarily better than talking to a lesser extent.

... ask your partner to tell you what his best times for communication are.

... identify your mate's favorite places for talking -- den, kitchen, restaurant or going for a walk.

... maintain closeness through brief notes or telephone calls rather than expecting your partner to engage in gabfests.

... initiate non-sexual, physical intimacy (hugs, kisses holding hands) in place of gab fests.

... don't reserve all your talking for your mate -- stay in touch with family and friends.

... find other hobbies and avenues to meet your needs for "entertainment" as writing, painting or playing a musical instrument.

... don't be threatened by your partner's silence.

... don't talk for him/her.

... remember that the lower communicator dislikes the "spotlight" just as the high communicator enjoys the limelight.

... use couple social activities to increase verbal intimacy. Date to relate!

When your "other half" likes to talk more than listen:

... remain an active listener without feeling that your partner requires responses, answers or solutions from you.

... develop tolerance and understanding of his needs to have an : "audience" to express his thoughts and feelings.

... refrain from criticism as "you talk too much"; all you do is say the same things over and over."

... don't feel you must participate in your partner's monologues or compete to talk more in dialogues.

... as a need for communication surfaces, ask that your partner "reserve" a time for you to talk at your favorite time and place.

... resist the temptation to criticize your partner's verbal interactions with others.

. . . remember that verbal intimacy enhances physical intimacy and vice versa.

If the intensity of passionate feelings alters with time and conflicts over different needs for physical intimacy occur:

1. Don't play the blame game. Remember a one or two point spread in Talking and Touching (Chapter V) affects a person's non-verbal communication.

2. Let your partner know if certain feelings (anger, boredom) are interfering with your desire for intimacy.

3. Improve intimacy through your social life. Use couple outings as a time to create physical closeness.

4. Increase closeness through non-sexual affection such as holding hands, kissing and hugging.

5. Develop a realistic physical intimacy script based on both of your T scores from Chapter V.

6. Let your partner know which specific intimacies you desire rather than giving reasons for not desiring intimacy. "I'd like a hug but I really don't feel like sex tonight."

7. Be open to specific intimate behaviour which your partner enjoys. Offer alternatives but only if you mean them.

8. Remember that non-sexual touching is inherently related to satisfaction with a couples sexual activities.

9. When a need for intimacy surfaces ask yourself what you really want. Is it a hug? A conversation? Physical contact? Intercourse? Then tell yourself (and your partner) what is the best way to get that need met.

10. Tell your partner if a particular intimacy is intended or not intended to lead to a sexual exchange.

11. Take turns initiating both non-sexual and sexual intimacy.

12. Never pretend that you don't have needs for attention when in fact you do.

13. Don't wait too long to seek professional advice if communication scores (from Chapter V) are two or more points apart or constant disagreements interfere with intimacy.

14. Remember, affection is important to both men and women. However, the quantity of one's needs is dependent on each of your T scores from Chapter V.

15. Remember that needs for physical intimacy do not necessarily lead to the demise of a relationship as readily as differences in needs for socialization.

If you have conflicts in decision making and problem solving (Chapter VI) and you are comfortable with your social life and verbal and non-verbal communication, seek professional help. Therapists help couples to face the problems of everyday life and at the same time, show them how to solve problems together.

If you are looking for ways to understand and cope with a critical or argumentative partner (Chapter VII) seek professional help. Therapists help couples to learn to deal with certain situations that make partners feel rejected, fearful and unliked.

Admittedly, almost everyone at one time or another, has found himself questioning his choice of partners and may even become fearful that his partner has doubts, too. But if it becomes necessary to arrive at a decision about the possibility of dissolving a relationship, overcome the tendency to consider only circumstamces rather than compatibility and the feelings or lack of feelings towards each other. Ask yourself:

- Do you first withdraw only to return and become emotionally involved with your partner again and again?

- Do "emotional ping-pong games", of confusion and uncertainty continue for weeks, months or years?

- Are you afraid to know if your partner still has feelings for you and you for him?

- Do you feel that one or the other of you emotionally withdraws from the relationship no matter how much the two of you try to maintain it?

- Have you considered that it is possible to be deeply in love with a totally incompatible person?

The ultimate decision whether to stay in a relationship in which one's needs are <u>not</u> and may not ever be met is more difficult since it is common to believe that the opposite of love is hate. The opposite of love is <u>indifference</u>. What is Indifference? It's when you no longer:

- are interested in what your partner thinks or feels.

- care to go out (refuse social invitations) as a family or couple.

- desire to do things for your mate (cook, wash the car).

- wish to have physical contact.

- react to your partner's promises to change, excuses for not changing or accept all the blame for the breakdown in your relationship.

- wish to make the relationship work.

- worry about the outcome of a separation and the possibility of an impending divorce.

In the end, there you are, standing outside your door, bags in hand, reiterating Clark Gable's famous one liner, "Frankly, my dear, I don't give a damn."

Chapter X

Two of a Kind: The Way It Was Meant To Be

Finding your perfect partner is like discovering a buried treasure. Is it really worth the effort to uncover the hidden traits of your ideal mate with whom you have an excellent chance for a lasting relationship before making a serious commitment? Yes, of course it is!

Things change when you shift the focus of getting acquainted from meaningless questions to relevant questions!

Whether you find yourself on a subway in New York, at the airport in Chicago, on the beach in Los Angeles or on a cable car in San Francisco, there are compatible people all around who could end up being your perfect partner. But in this era of disposable mates, it is up to you to have the right questions at your fingertips.

Why? Because "Some Enchanted Evening" you too may see a stranger across a crowded room . . . captured by those Mel

Gibson or Sophia Loren eyes and caught up in the magic of the moment.

How do you effectively pass from the usual "ice breaking" phase to the getting down to the brass tacks stage?

Once the attraction is there, it is inevitable that you will, in the fascination of a chance meeting, desire to know what you have in common. Are you similar? Compatible? Well-Matched?

Maybe you feel you would rather back off . . . it is too risky. He may be "turned off", walk away, or will not choose to respond. Do you pass up your opportunity to find out if you really are two of a kind? It is up to you! On the one hand it actually may seem risky. But on the other hand how many people do you meet that can pass your chemistry test in a week? A month? A year?

Questions! Think of one-liners for openers. Where are you from? What do you do for a living? Do you have any hobbies? Now that you have the formalities out of the way, you are ready to tap into those hidden traits usually left unexplored for too long. You will want to discover more about similarities between you and this mysterious stranger who passes your chemistry test and with whom you have briefly exchanged pleasantries. To do this, let us review the five other steps of the formula. It goes like this!

M: Mirror image: a similar personality type.

A: Activity level: an equal interest in socialization.

T: Talking and touching: a corresponding need for verbal and non-verbal communication.

C: Compromise: cooperative decision-making.

H: Harmony: mutual acceptance.

Remember all that glitters is not gold when searching for your ideal mate. The world is full of different types of individuals who will use one of four approaches to select partners: the methodical approach, the impulsive approach, the rebellious approach and the drifter.

The methodical individual plans ahead, has goals and is more likely to choose a suitable mate unless he marries for the wrong reasons.

Impulsive people act first, and often regretfully think over their choices at a later time. Ironically, their impulsive ways often find them selecting partners from one extreme personality type to the other, or reselecting their opposite type.

The rebellious person who is unlikely to heed warnings and unwilling to look inward, finds himself recklessly trying to fight the odds with near-matches and mismatches.

The drifter, always looking, aimlessly wanders from relationship to relationship often feeling empty, but carefree.

Caution: To know what type of approach applies to you is essential in mate selection. Be alert to the danger of meeting a compatible person with different goals than yours.

Moreover, there is a small percentage of people who have lifelong patterns that alter their decision making. This leads otherwise worthwhile candidates away from marriage altogether. Preconceived fears and anxiety impair their ability to make a commitment. These people need to understand and come to terms with these patterns which cause them to remain uncommitted.

There is a certain percentage of people who should not consider making a commitment without professional help: alcohol and substance abusers, spousal abusers, felons, those with debilitating psychiatric disorders and sociopathic personality disorders.

And now that you have a blueprint provided by the formula to guide you from dating to the kind of marriage everybody wants, you too can be a planner in your search for an ideal mate.

First, heed the previous warnings about conflicts which follow the coupling of opposite personality types . . . your near match or mismatch. But if, for your own reasons, you choose to continue a relationship with your near-match or mismatch in sociability and communication, you can do so at the risk of sacrificing your true needs for companionship and affection. Against all odds you can choose to wage this uphill battle on streets cluttered with heartaches and heartbreaks. It is your decision!

Remember that just because you know your own traits never assume that the person you first meet will necessarily know or desire to declare his own traits. There are those who unintentionally or deliberately create the wrong impression. Likewise there are private people who do not feel comfortable revealing their true personalities. But in more cases than not, you can count on an honest answer from the vast majority when you are attempting to meet and MATCH. They'll simply tell you the truth. Now, if you really are convinced after your minimal inquiries and heeding all the warnings that your newly discovered Mr. or Miss Wonderful passes your chemistry test and is your mirror image in both sociability and communication, you will be on your way to getting what you want.

As time passes, you will want to date as often as you can to learn how well you make decisions together as a team by freely sharing needs and resolving difficulties through cooperative compromises. To live in harmony as friends and lovers, be assured that you both like each other just the way you are. With your partner's approval you will feel understood, accepted and feel free to be yourself!

Finally, before your heart starts to sing "I love you truly" and "Can I have this dance for the rest of my life?" refresh your memory often by going over all six steps of the formula. Check for similarity and common denominators by observing your partner both at social occasions and private moments together. Occasionally, review the warnings.

If you feel you have made an honest appraisal of yourself and your partner and are realistic about your Matchability now - and only now - let your emotions flow. You have found a priceless treasure at the end of the rainbow - your perfect partner in an imperfect world. A long lasting love is your reward! This is the time to decide if you both are ready to make a serious lifetime commitment - Marriage.

Marriage is an unlimited partnership of love in which happy memories and warm feelings are stored up over a lifetime.

Think about what you want in a love partnership:

- Mutual desirability by which the sparkle of romance will be rekindled again and again?

- A mirror image with whom you can be yourself and still be loved?

- An ideal companion, enjoying and doing together?

- An intimate sharing, caring being?
- A cooperative, mutual exchange of needs?
- Living in harmony?

And now decide!

Profits of an Unlimited Partnership of Love:

1. Keeps love going and growing.
2. Emotional commitment.
3. See you through life's "ups and downs".
4. Conflict - ease.
5. Two of a kind.
6. Winner at marriage.

Dividends:

A storehouse of happy memories of being, enjoying and doing together - forever!

When you are with someone, and you are two of a kind that is the way it was meant to be.

Chapter XI

The Meet and Match Strategy

The Meet and Match Strategy section is designed to help you put the two of a kind theory into practice. Although the critical personality traits necessary for true compatibility usually emerge after the wedding ceremony and before the love relationship falls apart, you do not have to wait until then to make an intelligent choice. These are times when happy marriages are out of the ordinary, and divorce is an everyday occurrence. To help you to make a wise choice, I have prepared a series of charts related to the subject matter discussed in this book. This is the best way to anticipate the outcome of choosing a particular partner. Each chart is premised on the fact that the person you have in mind is one to whom you are physically attracted. Each chart is premised on the fact that as the relationship continues with that person who passes your chemistry, sociability and communication tests, you will determine his/her ability to compromise in decisions (C) and the degree of harmony (H) that exists. Choose wisely.

When Chemistry is Passed

SCENARIO	CHEMISTRY	SOCIABILITY /COMMUNI-CATION	OUTCOME
You have determined your scores in both Activity (A) and Talking and Touching (T). You meet an individual who passes on Activity (A) and Talking and Touching (T) and passes your Chemistry Test.	Passed	Passed	- Both you and your partner are physically attracted to each other. - Both you and your partner share similar needs for sociability. - Both you and your partner share similar needs for communication. - Compatible partners.
You have determined your scores in both Activity (A) and Talking and Touching (T). You meet an individual who passes your chemistry test, but fails your Activity (A) and Talking and Touching (T).	Passed	Failed	- Unfulfilled needs for companionship. - Unfulfilled needs for intimacy.

When Chemistry is Failed

SCENARIO	CHEMISTRY	SOCIABILITY /COMMUNICATION	OUTCOME
You have determined your scores in both Activity (A) and Talking and Touching (T). You meet an individual who fails your chemistry test, but who passes on Activity (A) and Talking and Touching (T).	Failed	Passed	- Lack of passionate sex. - Conflicts over sex life.
You have determined your scores in both Activity (A) and Talking and Touching (T). You meet an individual who fails your chemistry test, and fails on Activity (A) and Talking and Touching (T).	Failed	Failed	- Lack of passionate sex. - Conflicts over sex life. - Needs for companionship and intimacy unfulfilled.

APPENDIX A

ACTIVITY CHART 1

If you engage in a social activity one time per week, (A) = 1, and you meet someone who passes your chemistry test:

YOUR SCORE	MATCH	NEAR-MATCH	MIS-MATCH	OUTCOME
1	1,2			- Both you and your partner will desire to socialize one or two times a week. - No conflict over social life. - Needs for companionship fulfilled.
1		3		- You desire to socialize one time a week; your partner three times. - Conflicts over social life. - Needs for companionship at frustration level.
1			4,5,6,7	- You desire to socialize one time per week; your partner four, five, six or seven times. - Conflicts over social life. - Needs for companionship unfulfilled.

ACTIVITY CHART 2

If you engage in a social activity two times per week, (A) = 2, and you meet someone who passes your chemistry test:

YOUR SCORE	MATCH	NEAR-MATCH	MIS-MATCH	OUTCOME
2	1,2,3			- Both you and your partner will desire to socialize one, two or three times a week. - No conflict over social life. - Needs for companionship fulfilled.
2		4		- You desire to socialize two times a week; your partner four times. - Conflicts over social life. - Needs for companionship at frustration level.
2			5,6,7	- You desire to socialize two times a week; your partner five, six or seven times. - Conflict over social life. - Needs for companionship unfulfilled.

ACTIVITY CHART 3

If you engage in a social activity three times per week, (A) = 3, and you meet someone who passes your chemistry test:

YOUR SCORE	MATCH	NEAR-MATCH	MIS-MATCH	OUTCOME
3	2,3,4			- Both you and your partner will desire to socialize two, three or four times a week. - No conflicts over social life. - Needs for companionship fulfilled.
3		1,5		- you desire to socialize three times a week; your partner one or five. - Conflict over social life. - Needs for companionship at frustration level.
3			6,7	- You desire to socialize three times a week; your partner six or seven times. - Conflict over social life. - Needs for companionship unfulfilled.

ACTIVITY CHART 4

If you engage in a social activity four times per week, (A) = 4, and you meet someone who passes your chemistry test:

YOUR SCORE	MATCH	NEAR-MATCH	MIS-MATCH	OUTCOME
4	3,4,5			- Both you and your partner will desire to socialize three, four or five times a week. - No conflict over social life. - Needs for companionship fulfilled.
4		2,6		- You desire to socialize four times a week; your partner two or six times. - Conflicts over social life. - Needs for companionship at frustration level.
4			1,7	- You desire to socialize four times a week; your partner one or seven. - Conflicts over social life. - Needs for companionship unfulfilled.

ACTIVITY CHART 5

If you engage in a social activity five times per week, (A) = 5, and you meet someone who passes your chemistry test:

YOUR SCORE	MATCH	NEAR-MATCH	MIS-MATCH	OUTCOME
5	4,5,6			- Both you and your partner will desire to socialize four, five or six times a week. - No conflicts over social life. - Needs for companionship fulfilled.
5		3,7		- You desire to socialize five times a week; your partner three or seven times. - Conflict over social life. - Needs for companionship at frustration level.
5			1,2	- You desire to socialize five times a week; your partner one or two times. - Conflict over social life. - Needs for companionship unfulfilled.

ACTIVITY CHART 6

If you engage in a social activity six times per week, (A) = 6, and you meet someone who passes your chemistry test:

YOUR SCORE	MATCH	NEAR-MATCH	MIS-MATCH	OUTCOME
6	5,6,7			- Both you and your partner will desire to socialize five, six or seven times a week. - No conflicts over social life. - Needs for companionship fulfilled.
6		4		You desire to socialize six times a week; your partner four times. - Conflict over social life. - Needs for companionship at frustration level.
6			1,2,3	- You desire to socialize six times a week; your partner one, two or three times. - Conflict over social life. - Needs for companionship unfulfilled.

ACTIVITY CHART 7

If you engage in a social activity seven times per week, (A) = 7, and you meet someone who passes your chemistry test:

YOUR SCORE	MATCH	NEAR-MATCH	MIS-MATCH	OUTCOME
7	6,7			- Both you and your partner will desire to socialize six or seven times a week. - No conflicts over social life. - Needs for companionship fulfilled.
7		5		You desire to socialize seven times a week; your partner five times. - Conflict over social life. - Needs for companionship at frustration level.
7			1,2,3,4	- You desire to socialize seven times a week; your partner one, two, three or four times. - Conflict over social life. - Needs for companionship unfulfilled.

APPENDIX B

TALKING AND TOUCHING CHART 1

When Talking and Touching, (T) = 1, and you meet someone who passes your chemistry test.

YOUR SCORE	MATCH	NEAR-MATCH	MIS-MATCH	OUTCOME
1	1,2			- Both you and your partner share similar needs for talking and touching. - No conflicts over talking and touching. - Needs for intimacy fulfilled.
1		3		- Both you and your partner have dissimilar needs for talking and touching. - Conflicts over talking and touching. - Needs for intimacy at frustration level.
1			4,5,6,7	- Both you and your partner have dissimilar needs for talking and touching. - Conflicts over talking and touching. - Needs for intimacy unfulfilled.

TALKING AND TOUCHING CHART 2

When Talking and Touching, (T) = 2, and you meet someone who passes your chemistry test:

YOUR SCORE	MATCH	NEAR-MATCH	MIS-MATCH	OUTCOME
2	1,2,3			- Both you and your partner share similar needs for talking and touching. - No conflicts over talking and touching. - Needs for intimacy fulfilled.
2		4		- Both you and your partner have dissimilar needs for talking and touching. - Conflicts over talking and touching. - Needs for intimacy at frustration level.
2			5,6,7	- Both you and your partner have dissimilar needs for talking and touching. - Conflicts over talking and touching. - Needs for intimacy unfulfilled.

TALKING AND TOUCHING CHART 3

When Talking and Touching, (T) = 3, and you meet someone who passes your chemistry test.

YOUR SCORE	MATCH	NEAR-MATCH	MIS-MATCH	OUTCOME
3	2,3,4			- Both you and your partner share similar needs for talking and touching. - No conflicts over talking and touching. - Needs for intimacy ful-filled.
3		1,5		- Both you and your partner have dissimilar needs for talking and touching. - Conflicts over talking and touching. - Needs for intimacy at frustration level.
3			6,7	- Both you and your partner have dissimilar needs for talking and touching. - Conflicts over talking and touching. - Needs for intimacy unful-filled.

TALKING AND TOUCHING CHART 4

When Talking and Touching, (T) = 4, and you meet someone who passes your chemistry test.

YOUR SCORE	MATCH	NEAR-MATCH	MIS-MATCH	OUTCOME
4	3,4,5			- Both you and your partner share similar needs for talking and touching. - No conflicts over talking and touching. - Needs for intimacy fulfilled.
4		2,6		- Both you and your partner have dissimilar needs for talking and touching. - Conflicts over talking and touching. - Needs for intimacy at frustration level.
4			1,7	- Both you and your partner have dissimilar needs for talking and touching. - Conflicts over talking and touching. - Needs for intimacy unfulfilled.

TALKING AND TOUCHING CHART 5

When Talking and Touching, (T) = 5, and you meet someone who passes your chemistry test.

YOUR SCORE	MATCH	NEAR-MATCH	MIS-MATCH	OUTCOME
5	4,5,6			- Both you and your partner share similar needs for talking and touching. - No conflicts over talking and touching. - Needs for intimacy fulfilled.
5		3,7		- Both you and your partner have dissimilar needs for talking and touching. - Conflicts over talking and touching. - Needs for intimacy at frustration level.
5			1,2	- Both you and your partner have dissimilar needs for talking and touching. - Conflicts over talking and touching. - Needs for intimacy unfulfilled.

TALKING AND TOUCHING CHART 6

When Talking and Touching, (T) = 6, and you meet someone who passes your chemistry test.

YOUR SCORE	MATCH	NEAR-MATCH	MIS-MATCH	OUTCOME
6	5,6,7			- Both you and your partner share similar needs for talking and touching. - No conflicts over talking and touching. - Needs for intimacy fulfilled.
6		4		- Both you and your partner have dissimilar needs for talking and touching. - Conflicts over talking and touching. - Needs for intimacy at frustration level.
6			1,2,3	- Both you and your partner have dissimilar needs for talking and touching. - Conflicts over talking and touching. - Needs for intimacy unfulfilled.

TALKING AND TOUCHING CHART 7

When Talking and Touching, (T) = 7, and you meet someone who passes your chemistry test.

YOUR SCORE	MATCH	NEAR-MATCH	MIS-MATCH	OUTCOME
7	6,7			- Both you and your partner share similar needs for talking and touching. - No conflicts over talking and touching. - Needs for intimacy fulfilled.
7		5		- Both you and your partner have dissimilar needs for talking and touching. - Conflicts over talking and touching. - Needs for intimacy at frustration level.
7			1,2,3,4	- Both you and your partner have dissimilar needs for talking and touching. - Conflicts over talking and touching. - Needs for intimacy unfulfilled.

Notes

Printed in the United States
4757